LOVED BY Allah

30 Ways to Jannah

by

Salah Moujahed

Table of Contents

Preface

"(O Muhammad!) And when you make a decision, put your
trust in Allah. Verily, Allah loves those who put their trust in
Him."
[Surah Āl ʿImrān 3:159]

A re you loved by Allah (SWT)? Do you truly love Him with all your heart? How can you kindle the fire of divine love in your heart? And how should you behave to win the love of Allah (SWT) and delight it in your life?

"Allah loves those who turn to Him."
[Surah Al-Baqarah, 2:223]

To acquire Allah (SWT)'s love and His pleasure, our prime purpose must be turned towards Allah (SWT). This includes avoiding the things He prohibited, we should abstain from them. None of us is without shortcomings and sins, but our loyalty always must be focused on the one goal, which is to attain Allah (SWT)'s love. By constantly inspecting our thoughts, actions, and deeds and improving ourselves, we can become the person who is loved by Allah (SWT).

This book presents 30 ways revealed to us in the Holy Qur'ān that assist us how we can become a person loved by Allah (SWT), and the final result be the Eternal Paradise, The Jannah; this is the highest goal we can attain as human beings. In addition, it also explains the qualities and characteristics that are pleased to Allah (SWT), to incorporate into our daily lives and the qualities that we should avoid and restrain ourselves from.

"No soul knows what eye's delight awaits them—a reward for what they used to do."
[Surah As-Sajdah 32:17]

May Allah (SWT) bless us all with good health, unlimited happiness, patience, and strength. May all your wishes come true. May Allah (SWT) bless you with success in this life and with eternal life in Paradise, protect us all from the torment of the fire, Āmīn.

Your brother in Islam,

Salah Moujahed

Taqwa (Piety): Make Allah Your Shield

Taqwa is one of the most virtuous qualities a Muslim can have.

"The noblest and most honorable among you in the sight of
Allah is the one who is most righteous.."
[Surah Al-Ḥūjrāt 49:13]

The term Taqwah has been mentioned in more than 60 places in the Holy Quran and in over 150 verses in the Holy Quran, which deal with the virtues of Taqwah. For example:

"Allah accepts only from the people with Taqwah. "
[Surah Al-Mā'idah 5:27]

"The friends («awliya») of Allah are only the people with Taqwah."
[Surah Yunus 10:63]

There are various meanings and understandings of the word "Taqwah". It is often translated as piety or fear of God.

However, fear of Allah (SWT) is only one dimension of Taqwah. The meaning goes deeper, such as the linguistic meaning of Taqwah is shield or protective wall. It is about avoiding what displeases Allah (SWT) and not risking anything that will jeopardize one's relationship with Allah (SWT) and consequently, one's place in the Hereafter.

Some scholars had defined Taqwah as a protective cover between oneself and Allah (SWT)'s punishment. Taqwah means doing what Allah (SWT) had commanded and avoiding what had been forbidden, not out of compulsion but with a full heart. In our every step and action, we are mindful and aware of Allah (SWT), the Exalted, admitting His majesty and perfection by submitting to Him out of love, hope, and fear.

The reference to fear of God is found at the very beginning of Surah al-Baqarah:

"Alif-Lam-Mim. This is the Book in which there is no doubt,

a guide for righteous." **[Surah Al-Baqarah 2:1-2]**

Fear of Allah (SWT) in the sense of taqwah is not to be understood as a form of fear. It is rather in the meaning of awe of Allah (SWT) or as a worry that one will not succeed in attaining Allah's (SWT) love.

"So Flee towards Allah; verily I am unto you from Him a clear warner."
[Surah Adh-Dhārīyāt 51:50]

Therefore, whoever seeks Allah (SWT)'s love should not flee away from Him, but approach Him. If we see ourselves as creatures of Allah (SWT), then we should be aware that we were not created to burn in the torment of fire. Our task is to experience, learn and return to our Creator in this world:

"Many societies have passed away before you. So travel the earth and note the fate of the deniers."
[Surah Āl 'Imrān 3:137]

In doing so, we have been provided with everything we need to attain His pleasure. We just need to understand and use it as we make our journey back to Him.

In Surah Al-›Imran, a direct connection is made between the love of Allah (SWT) and the fear of God:

"Indeed, whoever fulfills his commitments and fears Allah,

Allah loves those who are pious."
[Surah Āl ʿImrān 3:76]

Therefore, whoever wants to be loved by Allah (SWT) should express it by his actions. The consequence of our sins is not much the punishment associated with them, but that we move further away from Allah (SWT) with our sins. If, on the other hand, we wish to seek the love of Allah (SWT) and return to Him, then it is advisable to refrain from all those things that may jeopardize that love.

"O you who believe! If you remain conscious of Allah, He will grant you decisiveness in separating truth from falsehood, and He will remit from you your sins, and will forgive you."
[Surah Al-Anfal 8:29]

In this context, Taqwah can be understood as the "consciousness of Allah (SWT)". It is the sum of the love and passion a person has for his Creator, for his Prophet Muḥammad ﷺ , and for Islam. By worrying about losing the love of our Creator, we show Allah (SWT) that being loved by Him is important to us. This does not mean that we only pray and fast, but that we simply avoid the things that are not pleasing to Him.

"O you who believe! Fasting is prescribed for you as it was prescribed for those before you, that you may become righteous."
[Surah Al-Baqarah 2:183]

The month of Ramadan is very suitable for renewing and strengthening our taqwah. However, fasting in the month of Ramadan is not primarily about abstaining from food and drink during the day.

Prophet Muhammad ﷺ said, "Whoever does not give up false speech (i.e., telling lies) and acting upon it (after Ramadan), God has no need for him to give up his food and drink (fasting)."
[Ṣaḥīḥ Al-Būkhārī 2078]

The more profound meaning of Ramadan is to gain Taqwah so that we become closer to Him. Taqwah is a reminder to us that Allah (SWT)'s kindness is always available for us.

Those who have Taqwah will get a way out of their troubles and relief in their affairs from Allah (SWT):

"And whoever has Taqwah towards Allah — He will provide him with a way out and will provide for him from where he never expected."
[Surah At-Ṭalāq 65:2-3]

"And whoever is God-fearing, for him He will make things easy for him."
[Surah At-Ṭalāq 65:4]

May our God-consciousness be strengthened, our hearts be purified by piety, our urge to please Him, and our love for Allah (SWT) be strengthened. For whoever wants to be loved by Allah (SWT) should show Him his love by committing fewer sins and trying to avoid mistakes. This is the concept of Taqwah and the most important step in finding Allah (SWT)'s love, for He loves the pious.

Taubah (Repentance): Repent of Your Sins

A s humans were created by Allah (SWT) and sent to this world (Ad-Dunyā), and He had given us free will, i.e., we humans had been given the ability to decide, and in doing so, sometimes we make mistakes. We humans are creatures who make mistakes and are imperfect.

Anas narrated from the Prophet ﷺ
"The Prophet ﷺ said: Every son of Adam commits sin, and
the best of those who commit sin are those who repent."
[Sunan ibn Majah 4251]

But Allah (SWT) had given us a great ability to repent on our mistakes and sins. So, asking for forgiveness is the true quality of being human.

"And (remember) when your Lord said to the angels: 'Verily,
I am placing a successor (mankind) on earth.' They said,
'Will You place therein those who will make mischief therein
and shed blood, while we glorify You with praises and thanks
and sanctify You' He (Allah) said, 'I know what you do not
know.'"
[Surah Al-Baqarah 2:30]

Allah (SWT) told the angels that He knows what they do not know. This means that although people would ‹do mischief and shed blood›, they would also repent for all their wrong deeds. In various places in the Holy Quran, the benefits, and virtues of repentance for people are mentioned.

Repentance is of paramount importance in Islam because it brings forth the love of Allah (SWT).

"… Verily, Allah loves those who turn (to Him) repentantly."
[Surah Al-Baqarah 2:222].

Allah (SWT) knows that we humans will make mistakes, but He also knows that we shall ask for mercy of those mistakes and promise not to repeat them. This will increase Allah (SWT)'s love for humans and bring us closer to Allah (SWT).

And not only do we make mistakes, but we even have to make mistakes to a certain extent to show deep repentance. The following tradition states in this regard:

Abu Ayyub Khalid bin Zaid reported:

> *The Prophet ﷺ said, "If you did not commit sins, Allah would sweep you out of existence and He would replace (you by) those people who would commit sin and seek forgiveness from Allah, and He would have pardoned them. said, "If you did not commit sins, Allah would sweep you out of existence and He would replace (you by) those people who would commit sin and seek forgiveness from Allah, and He would have pardoned them."*
>
> **[Ṣaḥīḥ Muslim; Riyāḍ Aṣ Ṣāliḥīn 423]**

However, this is not to be taken as a license to sin. Allah (SWT) warns us that despite the sins we commit, we should ask Him for mercy and show true repentance.

> *Say (o Muhammad), "If you love Allah, then follow me, Allah will love you and will forgive you your sins, for Allah is Forgiving, Most Merciful."*

[Surah Āl 'Imrān 3:31]

Islam does not recognize the 'original sin', as it would violate the absolute justice of God. We humans are responsible for all the sins we commit ourselves. Because if we were born with the original sin, we would make this as an excuse for our wrongdoings on the last day.

"O you who believe! Repent to Allah with sincere repentance."
[Surah At-Taḥrīm 66:8]

Repentance gives us an opportunity to wipe out all our sins from our lives. After sincere repentance, we are like a clean slate and can start anew. This is the true power of sincere repentance. There is no sin that permanently excludes us from the love of Allah (SWT). If we acknowledge our sins, truly repent, and turn back to Allah (SWT), then Allah (SWT) accepts our repentance. In doing so, we should never doubt Allah (SWT)'s mercy and forgiveness and strengthen our faith in Allah (SWT) as an all-forgiving Creator.

"Say, ‹O my servants who have transgressed against themselves:
do not despair of Allah's mercy, for Allah forgives all sins, He
is indeed the Forgiver, the Merciful.›"
[Surah Az-Zumar 39:53]

Sins that we sincerely repent of can even become good deeds.

"Except for those who repent, and believe, and do good deeds, to
those Allah will replace their bad deeds with good ones; Allah is

Forgiving, most Merciful."
[Surah Al-Furqān 25:70]

To understand that evil deeds can even be exchanged for good ones is related to the conceptualization of the word ‹repentance›. The Arabic term for this is 'Tawbah', and it also means 'return'. In the Islamic sense, it means to return to Allah (SWT) by giving up sins, accepting obedience, overcoming heedlessness, and turning completely to Allah (SWT), the Exalted.

Repentance thus means coming closer to Allah (SWT) than we were before our sins. Thus, there is only one small step that needs to be taken. Those who ask Allah (SWT) for forgiveness will change their lives, for Allah (SWT) loves those who turn to Him in repentance and in this way, human beings ascend even beyond the angels in status. We ask Allah (SWT) to make us among the Tawābīn, as He loves them who always turn back towards Him.

Ihsān (Excellence):
Strive for Perfection

"Ihsan is worshipping Allah as if you see Him, and although you do not see Him, you know that He sees you".
[Sahih al-Būkhārī 4777]

The Arabic word ‹Iḥsān› means perfection, excellence, or excelling oneself or showing competence. Ihsan is a derivative of the verb "aḥsanah", which means to do things better or in an excellency way and to do more than what is necessary.

Taqwah is the starting point of Ihsan, but Ihsan goes far beyond that. Compared to professional life, one would say Taqwah means service by the book: Tasks are done as required, whether fasting, praying or donating. Ihsan, on the other hand, characterizes the achiever in a business, the one who passionately and of his own accord performs excellently, much more than was required of him – and does so without talking about it, bragging about it, or demanding anything in return.

Even though we can never achieve perfection, we are still called upon to strive for excellence with all our thoughts and actions. We can demonstrate this through our inner faith (Iman) in word and deed, whether in work, social interactions, or our religious actions. This is Ihsan, the highest form of worship.

Ihsan can thus have entirely unique meanings depending on the context in which it is mentioned. Ihsan in connection with faith and Islam, refers to obedience and awareness of Allah (SWT). One who is aware of Allah (SWT) and knows that Allah (SWT) sees all our deeds will constantly strive to refrain from sins, intentionally and unintentionally, knowingly and unknowingly.

When the Prophet ﷺ was asked about Ihsan, he replied,
"Ihsan is to worship Allah as if you see Him, and if you do
not achieve this state of devotion, then (take it for granted that)
Allah sees you."

[Sahih Al Bukhari and Sahih Muslim]

Ihsan, without the direct connection to Islam or faith, means doing things excellently and simply being a good person, a so-called muhsin, a charitable or good doer.

"... Verily, Allah loves those who do good."
[Surah Al-Baqarah 2:195]

Those who strive for Ihsan in their faith, worship and daily activities and give more than is required of them will be rewarded with just that, whether it is success and excellence in this dunya, life in this world, or is about a higher goal. They will feel Ihsan in their heart, and their action will be rewarded immediately or later.

"Is the reward of goodness anything other than Ihsan."
[Surah Ar-Raḥmān 55:60]

Whoever recognizes the value of Ihsan and strives for it will be rewarded by Allah (SWT) in the form of Ihsan – the sweetness of faith, success in this worldly life, and ultimate success in Al-Akhira, the afterlife.

We can practice Ihsan in many everyday situations by gifting others and being good to them. If we are wronged, it is true that we are entitled to justice, which we can demand. However, personal excellence in the sense of Ihsan means that we can also show mercy and forgive our fellow human beings. Finally, we desire Allah (SWT) to forgive and pardon us. The Holy Quran states in this regard:

"The repayment of a bad action is one equivalent to it. But whoever pardons and makes reconciliation, his reward lies with God. He does not love the unjust."
[Surah Ash-Shura 42:40]

"... They should (rather) forgive and pardon. Do ye not love that Allah should forgive you? And Allah is all-Forgiving and Most Merciful."
[Surah Al-Nūr 24:22]

In other situations, we can learn to control our anger, rage, and resentment even when we should be in the right. We want Allah (SWT)'s full wrath not to hit us when we commit mistakes and for Him to be mild to us even though we may not deserve it. This is precisely what Ihsan is.

When donating and giving Zakat, we do not have to adhere to the mandatory minimum amount, but can be generous. When we realize that Allah (SWT) is the provider of all of us, we are not afraid to spend too much money on the needy. We know that Allah (SWT) will never let us become impoverished if we donate in His spirit.

For Allah (SWT) loves those who do good. Even though we will never reach perfection, we can still try to be a small step better each day than the day before. And we can ask Allah (SWT) to make us Muḥsinīn, doers of good, who find a higher level of His love.

Shukr (Gratitude): Be Grateful

G ratitude has a prominent position in Islam. It means thanking our Creator for all His graces bestowed upon us; thus, we express our gratitude by actions and deeds.

"… And whoever is appreciative is appreciative for the benefit of his own soul. And whoever is unappreciative (His favor), then indeed, Allah (SWT) is sufficient and Praiseworthy."
[Surah Luqmān 31:12]

It should be aware that it is not Allah (SWT) who benefits from someone's gratitude. We are benefitted from our thanks and appreciation of divine favors:

"So, remember Me, and I will remember you …"
[Surah Al-Baqarah 2:152]

Allah (SWT) loves our gratitude so much that He even guarantees rewards for it. When we show gratitude, we undoubtedly gain Allah (SWT)'s love:

For example, regarding mercy and forgiveness, it is said:

"He forgives whomever He wills, and He punishes whomever He wills."
[Surah Al-Fath 48:14]

"He provides for whomever He wills. He is Powerful, the Honorable."
[Surah Ash-Shura 42:19]

In the Holy Quran, we find many āyāt that elaborate on the importance of gratitude:

"If ye are grateful, verily I will grant you more ..."
[Surah Ibrāhīm 14:7]

"... But if you are grateful, He is pleased with you."
[Surah Az-Zumar 39:7]

So, there is no reason why Allah (SWT) should punish us if we act grateful to Him.

" What would God accomplish by your punishment, if you have given thanks, and have believed? Allah is Grateful and All-Knowing."
[Surah An-Nisā' 4:147]

Our gratitude and thankfulness to Allah (SWT) is the sum of this inner state and outer expression of gratitude by humans, which is called Shukr in Arabic.

The attitude of such deeply felt gratitude in our lives requires;

1. That we should attribute all benefits to our true source and not let anyone else share in them. For example, if we wake up in the morning without pain, this is solely the blessing of Allah (SWT). If we enjoy healthy hair, it is not the merit of our hairdresser or good shampoo, but it is a gift from Allah (SWT) who has endowed us with beautiful hair. The hairdresser may be able to help us take care of our hair, but this gift was also bestowed upon him by Allah (SWT). This attitude of gratitude must be depicted in all the big and small things in our lives.

2. That our heart is full of love and loyalty to our Creator, and we

also no longer hold grudges against His opponents.

3. That we should obey our Creator, who had provided us with infinite blessings, and heed His commandments and do not go against His instructions.

Unfortunately, there are only a few people who are paying true gratitude, while others are far away from the true essence of gratitude;

as The Holy Quran tells us in Surah Sabā:

"… Very few of My servants are grateful."
[Surah Ṣabā 13:54]

Yet, the blessings of Allah (SWT) that He always bestows upon us are so numerous that we cannot enumerate them completely. We are protected from harm of all kinds, have a wonderful body, the gifts of thinking, feeling, and many more blessings which are free for us, and the only charge of these blessings is worshiping Allah (SWT).

"And He has given you whatever you asked for; and if you (try to) count the bounties of Allah, you would not be able to enumerate them. Indeed, man is highly unjust and ungrateful."
[Surah Ibrāhīm 14:34]

Yet, it is so easy to gain Allah (SWT)'s love. By becoming aware of all the blessings, we are privileged daily and thanking our Creator for them, we not only give great pleasure to Allah (SWT) but ultimately to ourselves.

The Prophet ﷺ said, "Allah is pleased with a person who eats some food and then praises Him for it, or who drinks some drink and then praises Him for it."
[Ṣaḥīḥ Muslim]

When we say Alhamdulillah (all praises belong to Him), it is not just a simple thank you, but is rather an expression of gratitude to Allah (SWT) for all His blessings.

So, we should always be grateful to Allah (SWT) by saying Alhamdulillah regularly and remembering the source of all blessings and happiness in this life.

In difficult times, our gratitude is tested, such as occasionally, we lose a loved one, lose our jobs, fall ill, or suffer injuries.

The Prophet ﷺ said, "Strange are the ways of a believer for there is good in every affair of his and this is not the case with anyone else except in the case of a believer for if he has an occasion to feel delight, he thanks (God); thus there is a good for him in it, and if he gets into trouble and shows resignation (and endures it patiently), there is a good for him in it."
[Ṣaḥīḥ Muslim]

Especially in hard times, it is important to be relaxed and even grateful. After every difficulty comes to relief, and whoever remains patient and grateful to Allah (SWT) in difficult times will receive a great reward.

The Prophet ﷺ said, "Look at those who have less than you, and never look at those who have received more allowances than you. Then you will not disparage Allah's favor."
[Ṣaḥīḥ Muslim]

It is very essential that we remain modest in our expectations and value those people who have less than us. We should not compare ourselves with such people who have more than us, such as those who are more beautiful than us or smarter or richer. We should thank Allah (SWT) for all the blessings we have received because there are many people who have not been so richly blessed. Gratitude is the best way to please Allah (SWT) and win His love.

Moreover, it is not only for things or abilities that we should be grateful for. Often, we are also very particular about other people. We are unable to respond to other people's preferences and share our joy with them. This is a sign of selfishness, arrogance, and ingratitude. For example, some people think that they are not at ‹the same level› as others and cannot learn anything from them. However, this life is not about schooling or how highly graduated we are, but about experiences that we can share with everyone. Life experiences are important because they increase our knowledge. True gratitude, therefore, means feeling good in every situation.

May we always adopt an attitude of gratitude towards Allah (SWT), enjoy His blessings and praise Him for them.

Al-Hamd (Praise):
Honor and Praise Allah

The Arabic word 'Ḥamd' (praise) is not only an act of acknowledging and naming the good qualities of Allah (SWT). It is also carried out with a sense of love and respect, and it is an expression of praise with love, reverence, and veneration for Allah (SWT).

The Prophet Muhammad ﷺ said, "No one loves to be praised
more than Allah Almighty, and no one accepts more excuses
than Allah Almighty."
[Al-Mu'jam al-Kabīr 836]

In Islamic traditions, Ḥamd is narrated many times as Allah (SWT) loves to be praised, and He deserves all the good praises that we address to Him. Even if our praise is directed to His prophets or His creation, then ultimately, all praise returns to Allah (SWT) because He created all the things;

"Their call therein (Paradise) will be, 'Glory be to You, O
Allah!' And their greeting therein will be, 'Peace' And the last
of their call will, 'All praise is due to Allah, the Lord of the
Worlds.'"
[Surah Yunus 10:10]

As when our tongue is connected to our heart, and we mention Allah (SWT) and reflect on what we say, the praising of Allah (SWT) becomes a great act of worship and satisfaction.

Ibn al-Qayyim explained that Hamd is not merely the act of acknowledging, but it is from the deep heart with Mahabba (love) and Tadheem (respect).

In the tradition of Anas Ibn Malik, it was reported:

The Prophet Muhammad ﷺ said, "Allah will be pleased with
His servant who praises Him (saying Alhamdulillah) when he
eats or praises Him when he drinks."

[Ṣaḥīḥ Muslim]

To acquire the love of Allah (SWT) we must praise Allah (SWT) in all possible situations. Even after death, a true Muslim should praise Allah (SWT) because he is released from the prison of this worldly life and is heading towards the hoped-for life in the Paradise beyond.

Abdullah ibn Masud reported:

> *The Prophet Muhammad ﷺ said, "I met Ibrahim on the Night of Ascension, and he said to me: ‹O Muhammad, convey my greetings to your nation, and tell them that Paradise has pure soil and sweet water. It is a flat, level land. The plants grow there pronouncing, Subhan 'Allah, Alhamdulillah, La ilaha illallah and Allahu Akbar.›"*
> *[Jam'i Jām'i at-Tirmidhi]*

These four phrases are what Allah (SWT) loves the most:

- *Subḥān-Allāh* (Praise be to Allah / Allah is free from any imperfection).

- *Alḥamdulillāh* (Praise be to Allah / all praises are due to Allah / Allah be thanked)

- *Lā ilaha illā-allāh* (there is no true God but Allah)

- *Allāhu Akbar* (Allah is the greatest)

> *"Whoever praises Allah in this way will be granted rewards and his sins may be blotted out from his record."*
> *[Ṣaḥīḥ Muslim]*

Praising Allah (SWT) is especially recommended on almost all occasions, as the Prophet ﷺ set the best example and used to praise Allah (SWT) every time. This includes when going to bed, before and after eating or drinking, whenever wearing a new garment, or whether the Prophet received good or bad news. Furthermore, after waking up, when sneezing, even when beginning his speeches, after finishing his prayers, or when returning from a journey or pilgrimage, he never forgot to praise Allah (SWT).

The Prophet ﷺ recommended the following praises, among others:

- Upon waking **Al-ḥamdulillāh al-ladhī ʿāfānī fī al-jasadi wa-radda ʿAlaīyya Rūḥi.** (All praise is due to Allah (SWT), Who has restored my health and returned my soul) [Jāmʿi Jāmʿi at-Tirmidhi].

- On rising from a bow, as mentioned in Ṣaḥīḥ al-Būkhārī,

  Samiʿ Allāhu liman Ḥamidah (Allah hears who praises him).

- In prayer, as narrated in Ṣaḥīḥ al-Muslim,:

  Rabbanā Wa-lakal Ḥamdu abbana Walakal-hamdu

  (Our Lord, for You is all praise).

- When sneezing: **Al-ḥamdulillāh** (All praise is due to Allah)

In the following Ḥadīth, a dialogue with a companion of Prophet Muḥammad ﷺ as transmitted:

"We were praying behind the Messenger of Allah ﷺ one day
and when he raised his head from bowing he said: ‹Sami'
Allahu liman hamidah.› (Allah hears one who praises Him).
*A man behind him said, ‹**Rabbanā wa lakal-ḥamdu,***
***ḥamdan kathīran ṭayyīban mubārakan fīh** (Our*
Lord, for you is all praise, overflowing, beautiful and blessed
praise).›
The Prophet asked, ‹Who just spoke?› The man said: ‹I did, O
Messenger of Allah.›
The Messenger of Allah (ﷺ) said: ‹I saw thirty-some angels
rushing to see which of them would write it down first.› "
[Sunan an-Nasa'i 1062, Book 12, Ḥadīth 34,
transmitted by Rifa'ah bin Rafi']

How wonderful it is when we can praise Allah (SWT) in words that
astonish even angels. Of course, we can use simple phrases of praise.
But after all, we also love beautiful words. Such as, when a person
gives a gift to someone, they acknowledge it only with a simple ‹thank
you›, or he rewards us excessively with beautiful and sincere words of
thanks.

"And they will say, ‹All praise is due to Allah, Who has lifted
all sorrows from us. Truly, our Lord is All-Forgiving and
Appreciative.›"
[Surah Fāṭir 35:34]

May all our praises to Allah (SWT) be full of praise and gratitude
and be in the light and splendor of His perfection so that we feel true
joy in our hearts and the love of Allah (SWT).

Du'a (Supplication):
Ask Allah for Help and Assistance

Perhaps you know someone in your neighborhood who keeps asking you for something. You like this person and are usually willing to comply with his requests and help again and again. But as time flies, you get fed up and realize that you no longer answer the phone when you see his number because you know very well that the person wants something from you again.

But luckily, the divine principle is fundamentally different. Because despite how many times we turn to Allah (SWT) with our requests and seek His help, He never has enough of us; on the contrary, with every request we make to Him, we even come closer to Him.

The term Dua (pronounced Du'ā) has several meanings in the Arabic language, such as worship, seeking help, asking, supplicating, and calling.

So, Dua is considered as one of the best ways to connect one's heart to God and draw closer to Allah (SWT). Love for Allah (SWT) is the ultimate purpose of any dua.

According to Umar Ibn Al-Khattab, a dua is a servant's request to his master for help to support.

Allah (SWT) not only loves to be praised, but also to be invoked through sincere supplications. He also loves it when we are persistent in doing so, and He embraces everyone who tries to ask for His help.

> *"And when My servants ask you (O Muhammad) about Me, I*
> *Am near; I answer the call of the caller when he calls on Me.*
> *Therefore, let them answer Me, and have faith in Me, Perhaps*
> *they may be rightly guided."*
> **[Surah Al-Baqarah 2:186]**

The greatest mercy contained in this surah is not so much the answer we receive to our supplications, but the promise of Allah (SWT) to be near to us when we call upon Him. Thus, the real blessing is, as we know that Allah (SWT) loves to listen to us, even if we should have sinned or turned away from Him.

"And your Lord has said, ‹Pray to Me, and I will respond to your request…›"
[Surah Al-Ghāfir 40:60]

Another gift of practicing supplication is that we can be assured that Allah (SWT) will answer our requests in the way that is best for us, whether in this life or the hereafter. This may be immediately, in a few years, or only after our death.

Prophet Muhammad ﷺ *said that there are basically three ways when one receives the answer to a dua:*

1. one receives the answer or the result of the Du‘ā immediately in his life.

2. the Du‘ā is saved for a later, as yet unknown time in one's life.

3. one receives the answer or the result of the Du‘ā in the next life (Akhirah).

Du‘ā is the language of love for Allah (SWT). It shows Him our attention, builds a relationship between Him and us, and awakens our love in ourselves for Allah (SWT) Almighty.

Abdullah ibn Yazid reported:

The Messenger of Allah ﷺ prayed and said, "O Allah, grant me Your love and the love of those whose love will benefit me with You. O Allah, whatever You have provided me from what I love, make it a strength for me that which You love. O Allah, whatever You have withheld from what I love, make it a time of

rest in that which You love."
[Jām'i at-Tirmidhi 3491]

Love is an attraction between cause and effect. When we love Allah (SWT), it is because He is our source. And Allah (SWT) loves us because we are all His creations and thereby connected to Him. That is, everything revolves around the mutual love between us and Allah (SWT), the Almighty and Creator.

A powerful dua for Allah (SWT)'s love and mercy is:

رَبِّ اغْفِرْ وَارْحَمْ وَأَنْتَ خَيْرُ الرَّاحِمِينَ

Rabb-ighfir wa-rham wa anta khaīyrur rāḥimīn

"And say (O Muhammad), ‹My Lord, forgive and have mercy,
for You are the Best of all the Merciful.›"
[Surah Al-Mu'minūn 23:118]

Thanks to this dua, we can protect ourselves and our family from harm and keep negative thoughts away from us. It can be recited multiple times on any occasion. It will help us to love Allah (SWT) more than ourselves. Through our devotion and good deeds, we will also be showered by Allah (SWT) with His mercy and love, which will enrich our lives and lead us to our happiness.

Great Jihad (Effort): Purify and Make an Effort

"The Prophet ﷺ said: ‹Verily, the only reason I have been sent is for the perfection of excellent morals.›"
[Sahih al-Būkhārī, Musnad-e-Aḥmad]

The term ‹great jihad› (Arabic: Jihād al-Akbar) means the sincere effort in the way of Allah (SWT) (Arabic: Jihād fī sabīl Allāh), in contrast to the ‹small jihad› (Arabic: Jihād Al-Asghar), which is about militant encounters. It may seem surprising at first glance because a warlike dispute is given the attribute ‹small battle›, whereas the greatest battle we fight in life is with ourselves.

The following is exclusively about the great jihad, the goal of which is that we constantly try to overcome our emotions and wishes so that we get closer to Allah (SWT). Especially for our spiritual and moral growth, it takes many efforts to make progress. This includes our decision of which path to follow, purification of our soul, and our firm intention of wanting to continually improve ourselves.

> *"O tranquil soul! Return to your Lord, pleased and with (Allah's) benevolence. So join the circle of My servants. And enter into My Paradise."*
> ***[Surah Al-Fajr 89:27-30]***

The great jihad distinguishes three different stages of souls:

1. Stage 1- the bad soul: It keeps us away from Allah (SWT) and prevents us from purifying ourselves.

2. Stage 2- the questioning soul: It is better than 'the bad soul' because it always interrogates our actions and checks whether we are on the right path or deviated from it.

3. Stage 3- the contented and calm soul: It is clean, without envy and hatred and full of love for Allah (SWT).

Most believers have a questioning soul and want to reach the contented soul. The more we purify our soul, the more we can climb to the next level and reach the satisfaction of Allah (SWT) with our soul.

> *"The soul often enjoins evil, except for those on whom my Lord has mercy. Verily, my Lord is Forgiving and Most Merciful."*
> **[Surah Yusuf, 12:53]**

In our daily lives, even though we may have good intentions, but there are always some occasions when we are lured by Satan (Saīyṭān) to sin. In this way, we are controlled by our urges, inclinations, and desires resulting our soul is tempted to commit sins.

Although it is shameful if we create a distance between ourselves and our Creator through our misconduct, we should try to confront our desires and inclinations. Despite our sins, we can invoke Allah (SWT) again with a dua and ask for His assistance and mercy. This is because Allah (SWT) loves it when we strive again every time and try to do our best, even if we are not perfect and have sinned.

> *"… Verily, Allah loves those who turn (to Him) repentantly and who purify themselves."*
> **[Surah Al Baqarah 2:222]**

This verse refers to both physical purification and moral purification, with the aim of ridding oneself from impurities of all kinds.

The Prophet ﷺ said, "Do not underestimate anything among good deeds, even if it is only to meet your brother with a friendly face." **[Ṣaḥīḥ Muslim]**

We should not be ashamed of, if we sincerely repent of our sins, even if we had committed the same mistakes again and again. Only when we persist in our sins and make no efforts to purify ourselves, resulting us turn away from His love.

So, it makes a big difference whether we sin, realize it, sincerely repent and want to return to Allah (SWT). Or whether we commit sins, but our purification and striving towards Allah (SWT) is only half-hearted.

The Prophet ﷺ said, "Remember Allah wherever you are, and let every bad deed be followed by a good one to wipe it out, and treat others with excellent character."
[Jāmiʿ at-Tirmidhi]

Tawakkul:
Trust in Allah

"And when you have made up your mind, then trust in Allah;
for verily Allah loves those who trust in Him."
[Surah Āl 'Imrān 3:159]

The Arabic word 'tawakkul' means to trust in God or trust and firm belief in Allah (SWT). The corresponding verb in Arabic is wakala (وَكَلَ) and means to entrust, instruct, or authorize. Tawakkul describes the complete trust that Allah (SWT) Almighty is able, sufficient, and wise that we can rely on Him. In this world everything happens with His will and knowledge.

"And whoever trusts in Allah, Allah is sufficient for him."
[Surah At-Ṭalāq 65:3]

Tawḥīd is the foundation of tawakkul. Tawḥīd intimates that everything which exists is from the one and only Creator, Allah (SWT), and He is the only source of guidance. There are different levels of tawakkul:

The first stage of Tawakkul is to know Allah (SWT) through His attributes and qualities and believe that He is all-powerful and sufficient for us to rely on Him. He knows everything so that things can only happen with His will. We trust Him as we would trust a high-ranking representative (wakil). He is, in a sense, our supreme advocate. We make dua and repent. But when something does not go the way, we thought it would, we lose trust in Him and may search for an alternative (which does not exist).

The second level of Tawakkul is the belief that Allah (SWT) judges everything for us and takes care of all our worries and concerns so that we only have to wait for ‹a miracle to fall from the sky› without any effort on our part. The Arabic term for this is ‹Tawaakul (تواكل)› and not ‹Tawakkul›. The difference is only a letter, but tawaakul includes elements of laziness, inability, and a careless attitude. This contradicts every aspect of the life of the Prophet ﷺ. We should not be complacent or idle, but must do everything at our disposal to achieve our goals – entrusting ourselves to Allah (SWT).

Tawakkul does not mean that we can sit back and be idle, according to the saying, ‹I rely on Allah (SWT), He will take care of everything for me›. That would just be an excuse for laziness. For example, if we go into an exam without being thoroughly prepared and believe that it is in the hands of Allah (SWT) whether we pass or fail the exam, that has nothing to do with tawwakul.

The following ḥadīth explains what is meant by tawakkul;

Anas bin Malik transmitted:

The Prophet ﷺ was asked, "O Messenger of Allah! Should I tie my camel tight and rely (on Allah) or should I leave her untied and rely (on Allah)?" The Prophet ﷺ replied, "Tie it tight and rely (on Allah)."
[Jām'i at-Tirmidhi 2517]

Tawakkul provides a balance between our reliance on Allah (SWT) on the one hand and our individual responsibility on the other. At the same time, we are invited to join forces with a powerful ally, namely the Lord Himself, Allah (SWT). The more we rely on Him, the more likely we will also seek to please Him and follow His advice.

Even if we do not achieve what we originally wanted, we will not be depressed. And if we should succeed, we will not become haughty and arrogant.

"And Allah dislikes the proud snob."
[Surah Al-Ḥadīd 57:23]

The third level of tawakkul is the highest level of trust, which is complete trust in our relationship with Allah (SWT) and believing that all the matters of this world and the hereafter are in the hands of Allah (SWT). How could there be true love if there is still mistrust? At this stage, we realize that we can willingly entrust everything to Allah (SWT) and rely on Him alone. In doing so, we are content with whatever He has in store for us, secure in the knowledge that He will not cease in His goodness and mercy toward us and will see us through every difficulty on the way to His nearness and His love.

"If Allah supports you, there is no one can overcome you, and
if He abandons you, who is there after Him to help you? And
in Allah (alone) do the believers put their trust."
[Surah Āl ʿImrān 3:160]

So, we should always do our best of our ability, make all necessary arrangements, and then accept the consequences regardless of how it turns out. Even if we do not get what we originally wanted, then we should remember the following Surah:

"Allah does not burden any soul beyond its capacity."
[Surah Al-Baqarah 2:286]

As long as we do our best, we can count on Allah because whatever tasks we face, we will be able to pass them with His permission.

Ibn Abbas reported,

The Prophet ﷺ said, "Seventy thousand from my nation will enter Paradise without calculation. They are those who do not rely on incantations or believe in omens, but rather trust in their Lord."
[Ṣaḥīḥ Al-Būkhārī 6472, Ṣaḥīḥ Muslim 218]

Complete reliance on Allah (SWT) will steer us in a direction that is in our own best interest. After all, Allah (SWT) loves those who trust Him.

"So trust in Allah, for you rely on the truth that is manifest."
[Surah Al-Naml 27:79]

Sabr (Patience):
Be Controlled and Patient

"...Be patient; verily Allah is with the patient."
[Surah Al-Anfal 8:46]

Patience (Ṣabr) is associated with hope and trust in Allah (SWT) and is based on Taqwah (piety). Sabr is a quest that every believing Muslim should integrate into his life and adapt to different circumstances. The great importance of patience can be understood that it is mentioned more than ninety times in the Quran:

"The Prophet ﷺ said that patience is a light."
[Ṣaḥīḥ Muslim]

Light has the property of showing us the way and making us see clearly. We can only be truly patient when we realize that everything comes from Allah (SWT) and through Him everything is illuminated. It is the opposite of darkness and impatience. Impatience is darkness because it frustrates us, we act rashly and do not see the wisdom in delay.

"… Those who are patient will receive their rewards in full, without reckoning."
[Surah Az-Zumar 39:10]

The Arabic word Sabr also means to restrict or contain. It ensures that especially in hard times, our fears are contained, and lives are full of trials that we should face with patience, for everything comes in due time. Sabr also includes forbearance, endurance, determination, steadfastness, constancy and steadfast fasting.

Thus, there are various forms of Sabr known in Islam.

First, there is Sabr in the form of patience, as we usually understand it in everyday life. This applies to situations of anger, external pressure, confrontation as well as curiosity. But it also includes life circumstances that are beyond our control, such as illnesses, disasters, setbacks, or the death of a loved one. Despite our urge to react, to rush in and do something immediately, we remain reserved and reflective.

"A moment of patience in a moment of anger saves a thousand moments of regret."
[Ali ibn Abī Talib]

Instead of panicking and doing things that we regret afterwards, we first realize that all situations are part of our trial, and we must learn to deal with them. This is what we were sent to this earth to do. And our success depends on how we react, whether we panic, complain, bluster, get depressed, or learn to cope with difficulties. Although this kind of patience may often be difficult for us, it is only the lowest level of Sabr.

The Prophet ﷺ said, "And whoever remains patient, Allah will bestow patience upon him, No one can be granted a better and greater blessing than patience."
[Ṣaḥīḥ Al-Būkhārī]

The next level of Sabr is in the sense of forbearance, which we grant to ignorant as well as malicious people around us, whether they call us names, accuse us, slander us, mock us, disrespect us, or envy us, but we remain forbearing towards them.

Ibn Abbas reported:

I rode with the Prophet, and he said, "Know that there is much good at bearing what you dislike that support comes with

patience, and relief comes with grief. Trouble brings ease with it."
[Musnad Ahmad 2800]

Of course, we are entitled to defend ourselves against wrongdoing by others. The only question is how much attention we pay to them. Because in the pursuit of ihsan, we always have the choice to be merciful and to generously accept injustice.

" The repayment of a bad action is one equivalent to it. But whoever pardons and makes reconciliation, his reward lies with God. He does not love the unjust. As for those who retaliate after being wronged, there is no blame on them. Blame lies on those who wrong people, and commit aggression in the land without right. These will have a painful punishment. But whoever endures patiently and forgives—that is a sign of real resolve."
[Surah Ash-Shura 42 : 40-43]

The highest level of Sabr involves our faith. It acts in the form of constancy and perseverance with which we practice our faith in Allah (SWT) and obey His commandments.

"And seek help through patience and prayer; this is indeed difficult except for the humble ..."
[Surah Al-Baqarah 2:45]

If we exercise patience in worshiping Allah (SWT) and do not allow ourselves to be diverted from the right path to attain Ihsan in all our deeds, then this is the highest form of Sabr. We show Allah (SWT) that we are willing to be patient for His sake and strive for excellence so that our good deeds are accepted, and we prove ourselves worthy of His love.

> *"… and the angels will come in to them from all the gates,*
> *saying, ‹Peace be upon you for what you have patiently endured.*
> *How excellent is the final home.›"*
> **[Surah ar-Ra'd 13:23-24].**

Allah (SWT) loves those who are steadfast. A strong dua for patience is in Surah Al-Ārāf:

> *"Our Lord, grant us patience, and let us die in submission."*
> **[Surah Al-'Ārāf 7:126]**

10

Adl (Justice): Act Justly

The term 'justice' is found in 22 Quranic verses, which emphasizes its central importance in Islam. Moreover, justice is one of the attributes of Allah (SWT), and one of His 99 names is al-›Adl, which means ‹the righteous one›.

"…and Allah will judge everyone with justice."
[Surah Al-Ghāfir 40:20].

We often associate the word 'justice' with great rulers, governments or with a legal system that tries to make the coexistence of people in a state, or we think of the arguments of political parties that like to claim this term for themselves in their election campaigns, each in its sense and for its purposes.

Firstly, justice is a virtue that is good in itself. Other virtues, such as prudence and courage, are only good if they serve a good purpose. However, justice is by itself something positive, since it serves the inner quality of the soul and of society.

To establish peace and justice in a society, we need not only laws of justice, but also righteous people of justice. That is, justice as a virtue of political institutions should always be related to justice as a human character trait.

Justice, in the sense of Islam, goes far beyond institutions and apparatuses of power. It means ‹putting everything where it belongs› and takes place in all areas of life, business, family, friends and everywhere else.

The Arabic word for justice, ‹Adl› literally means to divide into exactly two equal parts so that there is no inequality between them.

The Holy Quran says that the entire universe was built because of a harmonious balance. We humans should not create any imbalance.

" And the sky, He raised, and He set up the balance. So do not transgress in the balance. But maintain the weights with justice, and do not violate the balance. ”
[Surah Ar-Rahman 55: 7-9]

Creating justice and equality in human society is harmonizing with what Allah (SWT) has already created in the universe. The prophets and scriptures were also sent down to create justice in society.

> *„"Verily, We sent down Our Messengers with clear proofs, and we sent down with them the Book and the Balance (of right and wrong), that humanity may uphold justice."*
> **[Surah Al-Ḥadīd 57:25]**

Before we perceive justice only in political systems, we are urged to do justice in our daily lives as well, to stand up for justice and not to oppress anyone ourselves. There should be justice in all our human affairs, including our family, our communities, our nation as well as the assembly of nations.

Thus, in our private lives, all children should be treated equally, whether boys or girls. In business and economic affairs, dealings should be fair and just. There should be no double standard in giving and receiving (see Surah al-Mutaffifin 83:1-3). In our dealings, we should speak justly (see Surah al-Anʾam 6:152) and not be influenced by self-interest or concern for one's relations. We should not be influenced by rich and powerful people or by compassion for someone's poverty (see Surah al-Nisa 4:135).

Anyone who violates principles of justice and even commits perjury or gives false evidence commits Shirk which is a great sin. This concept of justice and fair dealing is one of the cornerstones of morality that affects all people. Regardless of religion, race or nationality, people throughout history have admired and praised justice and fair play and despised injustice.

> *"Verily, Allah commands justice, and to do good unselfishly, and to*
> *be bountiful to one's relatives …"*
>
> ### [Surah An-Nahl 16:90]

Justice is a divine command and an essential part of our faith. As Muslims, we are required to be just and to act fairly.

Unfortunately, staying neutral and "outside" of a debate often seems to be the easier way to stay supposedly safe and guarded in a dangerous world. After all, if you are not personally under attack or oppressed, why risk anything for those who are? However, this mentality to protect ourselves will only hurt us more in the end. If we allow our fellow human beings to be oppressed, we are acting against the laws of Allah (SWT), for they are not in accordance with the meaning of justice. We make ourselves complicit by our inaction. Therefore, we must protect and support at all costs those who are oppressed or disadvantaged.

> *"O you who believe! Be upright to Allah and be witnesses of*
> *justice. And hatred against any group should not (lead you) to*
> *act other than justly. Be just, that is nearer to the fear of Allah.*
> *And fear Allah, verily Allah is informed of what you do."*
>
> ### [Surah Al-Mā'idah 5:8]

Righteousness requires a firm will and determination to be righteous to all people. Those who work for justice, even towards people they dislike, act entirely in the spirit of Allah (SWT) and deserve His love.

Justice also includes settling disputes and disagreements between two factions of believers fairly and justly.

"And if two groups of the believers fight each other, reconcile between them. But if one of them acts unlawfully against the other, then fight the one who is in the wrong until it submits to Allah's command. If it submits, then make peace between them in righteousness, and be just. Verily, Allah loves the equitable."
[Surah Al-Ḥujurāt 49:9]

May we always follow the path of fairness and justice, for Allah (SWT) loves the fair and just.

Sadaqah (Donation): Love Your Neighbors

Sadaqah (صدقة) means ‹voluntary charitable giving›. The Arabic term Sadaqah is derived from the root ‹Sidq› (truthfulness) because Sadaqah involves giving away goods and funds for Allah (SWT). It proves one's faith by one's deeds and thus by one's true inner attitude.

The Prophet ﷺ said,
"Sadaqah is a sign or proof of one's belief in Allah."
[Ṣaḥīḥ Muslim]

Sadaqah is not an Islamic obligation like zakat (obligatory tax) but a practice to help the poor or underprivileged. There is no minimum or maximum amount that should be given. And we should look carefully at whom we are helping and learn to recognize the truly needy.

"The needy is not the one who leaves when given food, but the needy is the one who has no money but is shy and does not ask for help."
[Ibn Kathir]

When we give to others, we show the strength of our faith and strengthen it.

"O you who believe, spend from the good things you have earned and from what We have produced for you from the earth, and do not choose from among them for donation the bad that you would not take for yourselves…"
[Surah Al-Baqarah 2:267]

Ṣadaqah in Islam does not only refer to money. Sadaqah can also be just a smile or kindness to a stranger, or removing an obstacle from another's path. Sadaqah is charity, helping others in any way we choose.

The Prophet ﷺ also said:
"Every good deed is charity."
[Ṣaḥīḥ Muslim, Ḥadīth 496]

Charity is more than just donating money. If we increase our compassion, love, and mercy to our fellow human beings, then we can receive the love of Allah (SWT) and His mercy.

The Prophet ﷺ said, "The needy is not the one who leaves
when given food, but the needy is the one who has no money but
is shy and does not ask for help alms (from what he earns)."
The people further asked, "If he can't even find that?" He
answered them, "He should help the needy who ask for help."
Then the people asked, "If he can't (even) that?" The Prophet
ﷺ finally said, "Then he should do good deeds and refrain from
doing evil deeds. That is considered a charitable deed."
[Ṣaḥīḥ Al-Būkhārī, Vol. 2, Ḥadīth 524]

If we do not show our mercy to our fellow human beings, whether family, friends, acquaintances or even strangers, how can we expect Allah (SWT)'s mercy and love to be bestowed upon us?

"Allah will not be merciful to those who are not merciful to
mankind."
[Ṣaḥīḥ Al-Būkhārī]

By serving others, we serve Allah (SWT). He makes us an

instrument of His generosity and mercy. Through us, Allah (SWT)'s work can work by not withholding it from our fellow human beings and letting them share in His love through our actions.

"You will not attain the virtuous conduct until you give of what you cherish. Whatever you give away, Allah is aware of it."
[Surah Āl 'Imrān, 3:92]

We can bring relief into the lives of our brothers and sisters in many ways: alleviate their hardship; soothe and comfort them when they are sad; assist them in sickness; boost their self-confidence; speak kind words to them; cancel their debts; share our gifts with them or simply give them a reason to smile.

"The parable of those who spend their wealth in the way of Allah is that of a grain that produces seven spikes; in each spike is a hundred grains. And Allah multiplies it to whom He pleases."
[Surah Al-Baqarah 2:261]

To gain Allah (SWT)'s love, we should be of the greatest benefit to all creatures of this world, whether human or animal and be kind, merciful, and charitable to them.

Abdallah ibn 'Amr reported:

The Prophet ﷺ said, "The Compassionate One has mercy on those who are merciful. If you show mercy to those who are on the earth, He Who is in the heaven will show mercy to you."
[Jām'i at-Tirmidhi]

Qu'a: Strengthen Your Faith, Body, and Knowledge

Even though we ask Allah (SWT) for His help and support, it does not mean that we humans are weak and needy. As Allah (SWT) has encouraged us to gain strength on all levels: spiritual, physical, and intellectual.

The Prophet ﷺ said, "A strong believer is better and more
loveable to Allah than a weak believer. And there is good in
everyone but cherish that which gives you benefit (in Akhirah)
Always ask Allah for help and do not fail to do so.
If you are distressed in any way, do not say, ‹If we had done
this or that, it would have turned out so-and-so,› but only say,
‹Allah has ordained and done it as He willed.›
The word ‹if› opens the gates of satanic thoughts."
[Ṣaḥīḥ Muslim]

Strength (Arabic: Quwwah) in Islamic understanding does not merely mean physical muscular strength but the strengthening of faith, knowledge, inner willpower, courage as well as physical health. If we want to improve and become stronger in all these aspects, it is to bring about good and earn the blessings of Allah (SWT).

The Prophet ﷺ motivated his followers by instructing them,
"Be eager for whatever is beneficial for you, seek Allah's help,
and do not be weak (in acquiring good)."
[Ṣaḥīḥ Muslim]

When we are emotionally, psychologically, physically, intellectually, and spiritually strong, we can help others and be a role model for others. In doing so, each of us is at a different level, so there should never be an excuse that we do not have enough ability. It would only be an excuse for laziness.

"He (it is) … Who created everything and determined its measure."

[Surah Al-Furqān 25:2]

We are challenged to become stronger in all aspects of our lives. In doing so, we can and should ask for Allah (SWT)'s help along the way.

Our body is a true miracle and a great gift. It has been entrusted to us by Allah (SWT) and all thanks are due to Him. We can show our gratitude for the care and attention we give to maintaining optimal health. By resisting temptations and not abusing our bodies (for example, by eating unhealthy food) or neglecting them (by not exercising enough) but keeping them in a healthy condition, we prove the strength of our will. However, a healthy, strong body should in no way tempt us to pride or arrogance, but rather increase our responsibility to bring about good and prove ourselves worthy of Allah (SWT)'s love. The Prophet ﷺ also praised health and even considered it more important than money.

The Prophet ﷺ said, "For one who fears Allah, wealth is not wrong, but for one who fears Allah, good health is better than wealth. And having good health is a blessing."

[Ibn Majah, 2141; Musnad-e-Aḥmad, 22076]

Physical strength and health also help us to approach Allah (SWT) by being able to pray, fast and perform Hajj. We can physically exert ourselves for Allah (SWT) and our fellow human beings, and much more. On the other hand, if we are physically weak or sick, then this is an obstacle in many good services that we could perform. And occasionally, we even have to rely on the help of other people. Instead of receiving, we should constantly strive to be a person who gives.

Even the daily performance of five prayers involves physical movements that use all the muscles and joints, which is beneficial for our bodies. Through our concentration during prayers, we relieve mental stress, which sometimes causes a variety of physical and mental illnesses.

Instead of us spending our time on distractions, we should strive to gain wisdom and spend our time on what is beneficial for us, as described in the above ḥadīth:

"Stick to what is beneficial for you."

However, this does not mean for selfish motives, but to be able to use our knowledge for positive things. When we gain knowledge and experience, we learn what is useful and what is harmful to our lives.

We all experience hard times. They are part of life. But they are only as hard as we allow them to be. When our will and courage become stronger than the nature of the problems, we can overcome anything with Allah (SWT)'s help.

In **Surah Al-Baqarah 2:286** we find a dua that gives us strength even in hard times, and increases our faith, and trust in Allah (SWT):

"Allah does not burden any soul beyond its capacity. He gets reward for that (good) which he has earned, and he is punished for that (evil) which he has earned. «Our Lord, do not condemn us if we forget or make a mistake. Our Lord, do not burden us as You have burdened those before us. Our Lord, do not burden us with more than we have strength to bear; and pardon us, and forgive us, and have mercy on us. You are our Lord and Master, so help us against the disbelieving people!"]

13

Haya (Modesty)
Be Modest and Humble

"*Allah, the Mighty and Exalted, is Forbearing, Modest and Concealed, and He loves modesty and concealment. Therefore, when any of you performs Ghusl (the general ablution), he should conceal himself.*"
[Sunan an-Nasa'i 406]

The Arabic word ‹Ḥayā› means modesty and natural or innate shyness. Haya further includes other values such as embarrassment, scruples, self-respect, shame, chastity, honor, and humility.

The Prophet ﷺ said, "Faith consists of more than sixty parts. And haya is one part of faith."
[Ṣaḥiḥ Al-Būkhārī Book No. 2, Ḥadīth No. 8]

Often, Haya is associated with the clothing of women.

"And tell the believing women that they restrain their looks and keep their modesty; that they should not show their beauty and adornments except what (normally) must appear of them."
[Surah An-Nūr 24:31]

However, haya is much more than the dress code of women and includes men.

"Tell the believing men to restrain their looks and to guard their privates. This will give them greater purity. And Allah is well acquainted with all that they do."
[Surah An-Nūr 24:30]

All the prophets and messengers of Allah (SWT) were on a higher level of modesty.

The Prophet Muhammad ﷺ said, "Verily, of the teachings of the first prophets who reached you is, ‹If you have no shyness, then do what you will.›" **[Ṣaḥiḥ Al-Būkhārī]**

Modesty and shyness in the Islamic sense mean that our soul shies away from indecent behavior. This quality prevents us from behaving badly towards others. It starts with how we express ourselves in words and actions: do we raise our voices to vent our anger, or could we restrain ourselves? Uncontrolled anger, for example, can lead us to insult or even physically attack others. This exposes our own bad ego and reveals our shamelessness.

The Prophet ﷺ said, "The strong is not the one who overcomes the people by his strength, but the strong is the one who controls himself while in anger."
[Ṣaḥīḥ Al-Būkhārī]

When we are strong in faith, we feel shy before Allah (SWT) and His creation, knowing that Allah (SWT) knows and sees everything we do. Therein lies the key to true humility. We shy away from being disobedient and feel ashamed when we sin or behave inappropriately, whether in private or in public. This kind of humility is haya, and it starts in our hearts.

The Prophet ﷺ said, "Modesty comes from faith, and faith is in Paradise."
[Musnad-e-Aḥmed]

Haya transcends shame and shyness and applies to every aspect of our lives. Haya inspires one to do all that is beautiful and refrain from all that is bad. Thus, it is a protection of chastity for our bodies and protection of purity for our souls.

Haya includes the way

- How do we dress: are we arrogant and boastful?

- What and how we say things: are we prone to exaggeration?

- How do we treat others: are we respectful and kind?

- What we do: are we doing good and giving our best?

- What we watch and read, e.g., movies, TV, shows, books: do these media demonstrate modesty as something worth striving for?

The Prophet ﷺ once said to his companions, "Be bashful before God according to His right to modesty before Him." The companions replied, "O Messenger of God, verily we are shy, praise be to God." The Prophet replied, "That is not it. Modesty before God according to His right to modesty is that you protect your mind in what it learns; your stomach in what it ingests. And remember death and the tribulations attached to it, and whoever wishes for the Hereafter, leaves the adornment of this life. So, whoever does all that is truly bashful before God according to His Right to modesty."
[Jāmʿi at-Tirmidhi]

Husn al Dhan: Positive Thinking

"Verily, thinking well of Allah is a part of excellent worship of Allah."

[Jāmʿi at-Tirmidhi 3970]

In our daily lives, we should also prioritize optimism by focusing positive thoughts on the attributes of Allah (SWT), on His blessings and miracles, and on our hopes for the Hereafter. By doing so, we can increase the effectiveness of our supplications and rid ourselves of anger, depression, and anxiety caused by worldly problems. As it is psychologically proved that our thoughts, feelings, and emotions affect our behavior, both positive and negative.

Thoughts come and go, but it is up to us which thoughts we attach importance to and pursue and which we ignore. The rule should be that we give attention only to good thoughts and refuse the other thoughts. Negative thoughts are thrown into our minds by Satan and never lead to anything good. To cancel their effect, we must replace them with positive thoughts.

Abu Huraira reported:

> *The Prophet ﷺ said, "Whoever believes in Allah and the Last Day, let him speak good or keep silent."*
> **[Ṣaḥiḥ Al-Būkhārī 6110]**

Our thoughts are positive when they evoke good feelings, inner gratitude, deep satisfaction, peace of mind, and good deeds. They are truthful thoughts about Allah (SWT), the Prophets, our blessings, or our hope for the Hereafter. They enlighten our hearts and enable inner wisdom.

Negative thoughts are associated with bad feelings, anger, envy, jealousy, greed, rage, hatred, fears, and other unwholesome emotions. If we only seek protection in the world and are mentally occupied only with it, we are constantly confronted with its deceptions. These include thoughts about money and our wealth, about our status, and about people we dislike or who have wronged us. Such thoughts arise from attachment to the deceptions of materialistic life in this world. They cloud our heart and prevent its purification.

Abu Dharr reported:

> *The Prophet ﷺ said, "Follow a bad deed with a good deed and it will erase it."*
> **[Jām'i at-Tirmidhi 1987]**

Just as we can cancel bad deeds with good deeds, we should follow bad thoughts with several positive thoughts to lessen their effect.

This does not mean that we should look at the world through rose-colored glasses. Of course, we must take care of our worldly affairs, pay bills, fulfil our obligations, and bear responsibilities. But it is up to us whether we get upset about situations in this world that are beyond our control or influence. It is better to focus our thoughts on the things that are necessary and useful. If we waste thoughts on a colleague who has angered us or complained about the suffering in the world that we are not improving, our attention is diverted from what we could change. Such worldly thoughts are of not useful for us. They are harmful and unnecessary.

An effective means of directing our thoughts in a positive direction is to think only about those things that should concern us.

Ali ibn Hussein reported:

> *The Prophet ﷺ said, "Verily, Part of the perfection of one's Islam is his leaving that which does not concern him."*
> **[Sunan Jām'i at-Tirmidhi 2318]**

Ibn Al-Qayyim writes in this regard:

"The most effective means is for you to occupy yourself with thoughts that should concern you and not with those that should not concern you. Thinking about what does not concern you is the door to every evil. Whoever thinks about that which does not concern him will miss that which does concern him."

[al-Fawā'id 1/175]

We can always turn our thoughts in a positive direction by thinking about all the blessings of Allah (SWT). This alone is an act of worship and gratitude, whereby we gain Allah (SWT)'s love and attract contentment and happiness into our lives.

Positive thinking also strengthens our prayers. A supplication that we recite with full confidence that Allah (SWT) will hear us is more effective and useful than a weak prayer. That is why the Prophet recommended that we pray to Allah (SWT) with the certainty that He will hear us.

The Prophet ﷺ said, "Invoke Allah with the certainty that He will answer you."

[Jām'i at-Tirmidhi 3479]

When we direct our thoughts in a positive direction, it brings forth our true faith. This means that we pray each dua with full determination in our heart and mind, while believing that Allah (SWT) has already heard and answered us in the best way.

The Prophet ﷺ said, "Allah says, ‹If he thinks good of me, he will get it. And if he thinks evil of me, he will have it.› "
[Musnad Ahmad 8833]

We can always expect the best from Allah (SWT) because every success comes from Allah (SWT), even if we do not know exactly what it will be. But Allah (SWT) knows.

"…Perhaps you hate something while it is good for you, and perhaps you love something while it is bad for you. Allah knows, and you do not know."
[Surah Al-Baqarah 2:16]

May we always be optimistic and full of confidence and not waste our energy on negative thoughts.

Akhlaq (Good Manners): Practice Noble Morals

The Arabic word ‹Akhlaq› (أخلاق) refers to practicing good manners, noble morals and attaining an excellent character. It is an essential part of faith for every Muslim. The following ḥadīth refers to the great importance of good manners:

The Prophet ﷺ said, "The most beloved of Allah's servants by Allah are those with the best characters."
[Ṣaḥiḥ Al-Būkhārī]

Exemplary and honorable behavior should be natural for every Muslim. After all, what good are all our prayers, fasting, and almsgiving if we do not behave decently towards our fellow human beings. This includes honesty, kindness, modesty, helpfulness, and truthfulness. In contrast, slander and defamation are particularly reprehensible.

A man came to the Prophet ﷺ and said, "O Messenger of Allah, there is a woman who is known for praying a lot, fasting, and giving alms, but she harms her neighbors with her tongue." The Messenger replied, "She is in Hellfire."
[Ṣaḥīḥ Muslim]

The Holy Quran also points out to avoid sinful words.

"Verily, successful are the believers. Those who are humble in their prayers and those who avoid from all empty talk."
[Surah Al-Mu'minūn 23:1-3]

When we discuss others who are not present, whether we talk positively or negatively about them, it is always a form of treachery or slander.

It was transmitted from Abu Huraira:

The Prophet ﷺ asked, "Do you know what slander is?" They replied, "Allah and His Messenger know best." He then said,

"It means saying something about your brother that would displease him." Someone asked him, "But what if what I say is true?" The Prophet replied, "If what you say about him is true, then you are betraying him; but if it is not true, then you have slandered him."

[Ṣaḥīḥ Muslim]

Backbiting and slandering other people are sins and keep us away from Allah (SWT). Regarding this, the Holy Quran states:

"O you who believe! Avoid most suspicion; for some suspicion is sinful. And do not spy on another, and do not backbite about one another. Would any of you like to eat the flesh of his dead brother? Surely, you would detest it. So fear Allah. Verily, Allah is Beneficent, Merciful."

[Surah Al-Ḥujurāt 49:12]

To receive the love of Allah (SWT), we must purify our souls. This includes ridding us of all bad habits of thought, speech, and action. Only then will our soul attain the receptivity necessary to benefit from the grace of our Creator.

Zaid bin Arqam reported:

"I will not say anything except what the Messenger of Allah ﷺ used to say. He used to pray, ‹O Allah, I seek refuge with You from incapacity, from sloth, from cowardice, from avarice, from old age, and from the torments of the grave. O Allah, grant to my soul the sense of righteousness and purify it, for Thou art the Best Purifier thereof. Thou art the Protecting Friend thereof,

and Guardian thereof. O Allah, I seek refuge in Thee from the knowledge which does not benefit, from the heart that does not entertain the fear (of Allah), from the soul that does not feel contented and the supplication that is not responded."

[Ṣaḥīḥ Muslim, Book 35, Ḥadīth 6568]

16

Latif (Meekness): Restrain Anger

"*Those who spend (in Allah's way) in prosperity and in adversity, who restrain their anger and forgive people, verily Allah loves those who do good.*"
[Surah Āl 'Imrān 3 : 133-134]

Al-Latif is one of the 99 names of Allah (SWT) and means ‹the kind› and ‹the meek›. In the Holy Qur'an and the Aḥadīth, the need does not give vent to one's anger but to remain meek and merciful is emphasized several times.

A man came to the Prophet ﷺ and said, "Messenger of Allah, teach me some words to live by. Do not make too many, lest I forget them." The Prophet ﷺ replied, "Do not be angry!"
[Sunan Abū Dawūd]

We all know circumstances in which we are angry and enraged. Yet, it is now common knowledge that anger, and rage are feelings like stress, can wear on the nerves and cause various health problems, especially if left unchecked. For example, blood flow slows, muscles and joints tense, and the cardiovascular system, nervous system, endocrine system, and brain activity are negatively affected.

While we know the importance of improving our character and embracing qualities of gentleness, humility, patience, and forgiveness, but along the way, in our daily lives, we repeatedly encounter the difficulty of how to restrain and control ourselves when anger rises within us.

The first thing that is helpful is to think immediately, at the first sign of anger, about why the anger is occurring and whether it is necessary to be angry. We should direct this question not to other people but to Allah (SWT), thinking of the Hereafter (Akhirah). This idea alone makes us realize how significant or insignificant the cause of our anger may be and puts the situation into perspective.

The Messenger of Allah ﷺ teaches us to control our anger in

various aḥadīth.

The Prophet ﷺ said, "I know a sentence. If he utters it, it will make him relax. If he says, ‹I seek refuge with Allah from Satan› then all his anger will go away."
[Ṣaḥiḥ Al-Būkhārī ; Vol. 4, No. 502 and Sunan Abu Dawud; Book 41, No. 4762]

A powerful key to controlling our anger is to seek refuge from Satan in Allah (SWT). This is because Satan is an enemy of human beings who promotes evil between them and manipulates their personal perceptions through whispers. Satan does everything he can to ensure that there is strife and misunderstanding between people. We should be aware of this. This is also emphasized in the following verse:

"And say to My servants, let them speak only what is best; for Satan sows discord among them. Verily, Satan is a open enemy to man."
[Surah Al-Isra" 17:53]

The manipulations by Satan are devious. Occasionally, it is just a single word that has been misinterpreted or misunderstood. And there is already a conflict that affects the relationship between friends, acquaintances, or family members. This can sometimes drag on for years, to the point that people stop talking to each other because of it.

Another tip to control one's anger is given by the following ḥadīth, which recommends ablution.

*"Anger comes from the devil, the devil was created of fire,
and fire can be extinguished with water; so, when one of you
becomes angry, he should perform ablution."*
[Sunan Abu Dawud; Book 41, No. 4766]

When we are angry, words come across our lips that we may regret
afterwards, and we cannot undo them. Therefore, the following ḥadīth
is also very helpful:

*The Prophet ﷺ said, "If one of you becomes angry, he should
keep silent."*
**[Ṣaḥiḥ Al-Būkhārī, Ḥadīth 245 and
Musnad Ahmad]**

This also applies in circumstances where we are trying to settle a
dispute between two people or when we are supposed to pronounce
judgment as a judge. If we are in a state of anger, it is better to remain
silent and only speak when the anger has fully subsided.

Abu Bakr wrote to his son:

*"Do not judge between two people when you are in an angry
mood, for I heard the Prophet ﷺ say: ‹A judge should not judge
between two people while he is in an angry mood.› "*
[Ṣaḥiḥ Al-Būkhārī Vol. 9, No. 272]

Our body posture also has a great effect when we have negative
emotions. Thus, sometimes when we deliver bad news, we instinctively
say, ‹Sit down first.›

Abu Dharr reported:

The Prophet ﷺ said to us, "If one of you becomes angry while standing, he should sit down.› If the anger leaves him, well and good; otherwise he should lie down."
[Sunan Abu Dawud, Book 41, No. 4764]

If we feel anger towards our fellow human beings, we cannot possibly be merciful. How can we expect mercy from Allah (SWT)?

The Prophet ﷺ said, "Whoever does not show mercy to people, Allah will not show mercy to him (either)."
[Ṣaḥiḥ Al-Būkhārī and Ṣaḥīḥ Muslim]

This shows how important it is that we do not hurt our brothers and sisters in the first place. And if we ourselves have been hurt, for Allah (SWT), we should show patience and be willing to forgive. This is the mercy we hope to receive from Allah (SWT).

The Prophet ﷺ said, "Verily, Allah is gentle, and He loves gentleness. He rewards for gentleness what is not granted for harshness, and He rewards nothing else."
[Ṣaḥīḥ Muslim 2593]

The following dua of the Prophet ﷺ was transmitted by Ammar Bin Yaasir and reported by Imam an-Nasaa'i:

"I ask you, O Allah, for truthful speech in times of joy and anger."
[Nasaa'i No. 1305; Sahih Al-Jaami No. 1301]

17

Khushu (Humility): Discard Pride and Arrogance

"*And seek help through patience and prayer; this is indeed difficult except for the humble.*"
[Surah Al-Baqarah 2:45]

The term humility is often misunderstood in our society today and equated with oppression and humiliation. Consequently, people who are humble and openly show it to the outside world are considered weak, as it seems to compromise their personal dignity. At times, truly humble people even risk exposing themselves to the ridicule of others.

However, true humility has another meaning. Humility is the opposite of haughtiness, overconfidence, arrogance, and pride. It is a form of respect and gratitude. A humble person puts aside his pride and recognizes his limitations. He knows the value of others and the value of even seemingly small things, be it a flower, a stone, a drop of water or a butterfly. He does not need to demean other things or look down on others to elevate himself, recognizing that everything in this world is unique and endowed with special talents.

There is no need to overestimate one's own ability or achievements and to take oneself too seriously. However, this does not mean despising or devaluing oneself. This would otherwise be a misconceived humility.

Iyad ibn Himar reported:

The Messenger of Allah ﷺ said, "Verily, Allah has revealed to me that you should adopt humility. So that no one will wrong another, and no one will be disdainful and haughty towards another."

[Ṣaḥīḥ Muslim]

Humility involves trusting in Allah, for humility is not only for the creation down to the smallest detail but even more so for its Creator, who created all this. We voluntarily submit to Him and show our submission to Him because we recognize His magnificence and are aware of our limitations. There is no need for pride, vanity, or arrogance because trusting in Allah, there is no need to worry that we will fall short or be deprived.

Humility leads to the love of Allah (SWT) and entry into Paradise, while arrogance leads to the displeasure of Allah (SWT) and may lead to hell.

> *"Call upon your Lord humbly and privately. He does not love*
> *the aggressors. And do not make mischief in the earth after it*
> *has been set in order! And call upon Him in fear and hope.*
> *Verily, Allah's mercy is near to those who do good works."*
> ***[Surah Al-'Ārāf 7: 55-56]***

Humility involves acting selflessly and putting oneself aside without seeking public recognition and flaunting it. Only those who develop true humility can achieve true piety or righteousness. Humility is one of the noblest characteristics we humans can adopt.

> *"O you who believe! Kneel, and prostrate, and worship your*
> *Lord and do good deeds, that you may succeed."*
> ***[Surah Al-Hajj 22:77]***

In the following ḥadīth, it was narrated that Allah (SWT) elevates those who show humility.

Abu Said al-Khudri reported:

> *The Messenger of Allah ﷺ said,*
> *"Whoever humbles himself by one step for Allah, Glory be to*
> *Him, Allah will elevate him by one step. Whoever is arrogant*
> *towards Allah by one step, Allah will lower him by one step*

until he is the lowest of the low."
[Sunan ibn Majah 4176]

The Prophet ﷺ also said, "It is a right from Allah that nothing in the world will be elevated (in greatness or esteem) except that Allah will bring it down."
[Ṣaḥīḥ Al-Būkhārī]

When we seek the benefits of the world or the hereafter, part of our success lies in our ability to humble ourselves in our search. For example, if someone is seeking knowledge, they must humble themselves in their struggle and effort to achieve this goal.

"The believers are only those who believe in Allah and His Messenger, and then have not doubted (their faith) and devote their possessions and their lives to Allah's cause. These are the truthful ones."
[Surah Al-Ḥujurāt 49:15]

18

Hilm (Forbearance): Be Forbearing and Prudent

Linguistically, the Arabic word Hilm means forbearance, and implies an understanding of people's imperfections. Forbearance is the ability to look upon others for their faults and weaknesses and to regard them with compassion and love. Although the term Hilm has not been explicitly used in the Holy Quran, its derivatives (Al-Ḥalīm)

have been mentioned several times.

First, it is important to understand the difference between forbearance (ḥilm) and patience (sabr). A patient person (Arabic: Ṣābir) suppresses his inner urge to burst into anger or despair, whereas a forbearing person (Arabic: Ḥalīm) is inwardly composed, calm, and at peace. Moreover, the two qualities differ in that an indulgent person would also be able to put the other person in his place. This is not necessarily the case with a patient person. The following ayah includes both of Allah (SWT)'s attributes, His forbearance and His patience:

"And do not ever think that Allah is unaware of what the wrongdoers do. He only defers them a respite until the Day when the eyes will gaze fixedly."
[Surah Ibrāhīm 14:42]

Al-Halim (the forbearing) is one of the 99 names of Allah. The Tafsir al-Sa'di states:

"Al-Halim (the Forbearing) is He Who keeps bestowing blessings on His creation, visible and hidden, despite their sins and many missteps. So, He shows forbearance by not punishing the sinners, but always encouraging them to repent and giving them time to humble themselves before Him."

Allah (SWT) has complete knowledge and power over us. And yet, He shows us His love by always giving us respite to mend our ways. He knows the behavior of people who betray Him, slanders Him, and even flaunt their bad behavior. However, instead of punishing them, He allows their lungs to continue breathing, their hearts to beat, and their supplies to be provided.

> *"Verily, Allah holds the heavens and the earth so that they do*
> *not depart. And if they were to fall apart, there would be none*
> *but He to hold them. Verily, He is Forbearing, All-Forgiving."*
> **[Surah Fāṭir 35:41]**

If we imagine in our mind's eye how many sins are committed against this wonderful creation of Allah (SWT) every day, how many murders, thefts, idolatrizes and perversions of all kinds happen, then it almost borders on a miracle when the sun rises again tomorrow, and we are allowed to admire the beauty of the stars at night. And we can ask ourselves what the world would be like without the forbearance of Allah (SWT) to get an idea of the love we are showered with.

> *"And if Allah punished the people for all that they do, He*
> *would not leave a living creature on the (earth's) surface; but He*
> *grants them respite until a certain term; and when their term is*
> *up, Allah is observant of His servants."*
> **[Surah Fāṭir 35:45]**

Allah (SWT) is not only Al-Ḥalīm, but He also loves those who have qualities of Halim. The ability to be lenient towards one's fellow human beings and not to be upset even in the face of injustice proves a person's righteousness. It is therefore one of the most important qualities of a believing Muslim. A believer is aware of people's imperfections and weaknesses and remains peaceful without any desire for revenge or anger. However, this does not mean showing leniency in the face of injustice. That would be weakness and cowardice.

The ability to Hilm is rewarded with the love of Allah (SWT). Ibn Abbas transmitted that the Prophet ﷺ said to Ashajj Abdul-Qais,

"Indeed, there are two qualities in you that Allah loves: forbearance and prudence."
[Jāmi' at-Tirmidhi 2011, Book 27, Ḥadīth 117]

In this ḥadīth, reference has been made to another significant quality that finds Allah (SWT)'s favor and love, namely the ability to be prudent. Unfortunately, this is increasingly lost in today's fast-paced world. We rush from one deadline to the next, no longer giving the individual tasks the necessary calm and deliberation. But only when we have control over ourselves and our environment and approach things in a structured and level-headed way, we can make progress. This does not mean being slow, but making sure that we do not rush things and are not hasty and do our important matters correctly.

The Prophet ﷺ said, "Prudence is from Allah, while haste is from Shaitan (Satan). There is no one who grants more excuses than Allah, and there is no quality that Allah loves more than Hilm."
[Abu Huraira via Shu'b al Iman]

Forbearance and prudence have the same origin. Both spring from a sense of inner peace and the certainty of being on the path toward Allah (SWT). In such a state of mind, it can bounce off us whether people try to insult us, put us stressed, or lead us into negative actions because we see this only as external trials that lie in our path.

> *"Hilm is the restraint of one's self and one's nature from the outbursts of anger."*
> ### *[Al-Mufrādāt]*

You can think of it as being in a large marketplace, and you know at 6 pm it will close. The goal is to have collected as many good qualities as possible by then. Only then will you find the right exit. Now it is up to everyone what he does with his time and has collected by 6 pm. One person will have nothing at all in his basket because he has been seduced by the great offer and has wasted his time with games, quarrels, useless bustle, anger, and annoyance. And someone else's basket is filled with many positive achievements such as patience, determination, focus on important things, mindfulness, kindness, and love. There was no room in his basket for other people's insults and annoyances. The latter has a much better chance of being shown the correct exit door of the marketplace.

We can bring Hilm into all aspects of our lives, whether as a parent, a spouse, a friend, in business or in education towards other students or teachers. Without forbearance and prudence, no relationship, friendship, or successful business will last. Positive leadership qualities are also associated with Hilm.

Certainly, we cannot be Halim overnight, but practice makes perfect, as we all know. Just like our physical development, the development of our morals takes time. But whoever takes up this task will be rewarded by Allah (SWT).

Abu Huraira reported:

The Prophet ﷺ said, "Verily, knowledge comes only by learning and forbearance comes only by cultivating forbearance. Whoever strives for good will receive good, and whoever avoids evil will be saved from it."
[Tārikh Baghdad 9/129]

Forbearance and prudence are great virtues to strive for. With patience, prudence, and concentration on this goal, we can develop Hilm within us.

19

Muraqabah (Mindfulness): Train Your Spirit

Mindfulness means focusing our attention on the experiences and perceptions in the here and now, without the hastily evaluating or judging them. It is a special kind of attention that allows us to register and allow inner and outer experiences in the present moment without prejudice.

Our modern life is filled with hustle and bustle, noise, distraction, information overload, anxiety, and worry. Our senses are constantly stimulated so that even a small moment of silence becomes increasingly rare for some of us. A permanent inner turmoil prevents us from making the most of every moment. It also reduces the quality of our prayers and our ability to remember Allah (SWT), as our thoughts and desires constantly wander back and forth.

Cultivating mindfulness in our lives brings measurable benefits to health and well-being. It helps us reduce stress, strengthen our memory, improve our concentration, better control emotions, and strengthen our personal relationships. Likewise, it enhances our empathy and compassion for others.

We can also achieve positive developments in our spiritual practice through mindfulness. The Islamic concept of practicing mindfulness is called Muraqabah (Arabic: مراقبة). It means ‹to observe attentively›. Muraqabah helps us train our mind and discipline and focus on our connection with Allah (SWT).

Muraqabah involves mindfulness of all our intentions, thoughts, emotions, and inner states by becoming aware of the thoughts we pursue and the words we speak.

Ibn al-Qayyim said,

> *"… Muraqabah is not simply a recommended character*
> *trait, but rather the realization of the highest character trait,*
> *spiritual excellence (al-Ihsan). As the Prophet ﷺ said, spiritual*
> *excellence means ‹worshiping Allah as if we see Him, for even*
> *if we do not see Him, He certainly sees us.›"*
> **[Ṣaḥīḥ Al-Bukhārī]**

"He knows what enters the earth and what comes out of it,
what descends from the sky and what ascends to it. And He is
with you wherever you are. And Allah sees all that you do."
[Surah Al-Ḥadīd 57:4]

Muraqabah always helps us on our way towards spiritual excellence by being fully aware of Allah (SWT). This is mindfulness in the sense of muraqabah and the epitome of faith. The reward of muraqabah, apart from the prospect of eternal life in Paradise, is a state of calm serenity that leads to contentment in our earthly lives. This also makes us understand fate (qadrr) as something positive.

The following ḥadīth teaches us how to live a peaceful and happy life by paying attention to Allah (SWT), trusting Him completely and worshiping Him.

Abu Al-Abbas-Abdullah-Bin-Abbas reported:

One day, I was behind the Prophet ﷺ, and he said to me,
"O young man, I will teach you some words: Be mindful of
Allah, and Allah will protect you. Remember Allah, and you
will find Him before you. If you need to ask, then ask Allah,
and if you seek help, then seek help from Allah. Know that
even if the people (or the whole community) were to gather
to do you some good, they would not do you any good except
what Allah has already written down for you. And that if they
were to gather to do you harm, they could not do you any harm
except what Allah has already written down against you. The
(writing) feathers were erected, and the pages dried."
[Jāmᶜi at-Tirmidhi 2516]

To practice mindfulness, it is helpful to be in a state of silence. Silence is the preferred state of being in which we are not distracted by the noise of the world. This includes being silent ourselves. If we have nothing good to say, it is better to be silent and think over our words beforehand.

The Prophet ﷺ said, "Whoever believes in Allah and the Last Day, let him speak good or keep silent."
[Ṣaḥīḥ Al-Būkhārī , 8:100, No. 6475]

Silence has a great effect on our heart and character because the habit of speaking badly or carelessly leads to an impure heart. Our words and our heart are connected. When we guard our tongue, we also guard our heart.

The Prophet ﷺ said, "A servant's faith is not sincere until his heart is sincere, and his heart is not sincere until his tongue is sincere."
[Ibn Hanbal, Ahmad; Ibn Taymiyyah]

Therefore, we must not only tolerate silence, but enjoy silence and consider it as developing a positive character. We can increase our mindfulness of Allah (SWT) and our own inner state of existence in silence. The ability to be silent also tends to be a sign of a wise person.

Abu Darda› al-Ansari said,

"Silence is a form of wisdom, but few people practice it."

Silence is closely related to muraqabah. In silence, we can direct our awareness to the here and now, abandon preoccupation with the past and future, and limit it to what is necessary and useful. A close companion of tranquility is seclusion to worship Allah (SWT) alone in peace

> *The Prophet ﷺ said, "The secluded ones (al-mufarridun) ran*
> *ahead." They asked, "O Messenger of Allah, who are the*
> *departed?" The Prophet ﷺ replied, "They are men and women*
> *who remember Allah often."*
> **[Ṣaḥīḥ Muslim]**

If we often think about the world and all its shortcomings, it leads to unhappiness and impure hearts. It weakens our mindfulness and our hope in Allah (SWT), which encourages us to do good deeds. And it diminishes our reverence for Allah (SWT), which keeps us from sinning.

Ismail ibn Ibrahim al-Nasrabadhi said:

> *"Hope motivates you to obey, fear keeps you from disobedience,*
> *and muraqabah guides you to the path of truth."*
> **[Al-Qushayri, Al-Risala al-Qushayriyya 1:331]**

By remembering and being aware of Allah (SWT), we can purify our hearts. Man has the peculiarity that he can only think of one thing at a time. We can take advantage of this phenomenon because we cannot think of Allah (SWT) and the world at the same time.

*Ibn Al-Qayyim explained, ‹that our preparation for the hereafter
is to reflect (tafakkur), remember (tadhakkur), investigate
(nathr), reflect (ta'amul), ponder (i'tibar), consider (tadabbur),
and ruminate (istibsar).›*

These terms are all mental activities, some of which overlap, but some of which are subtly different. They can be thought of as forms of meditation.

When we take a certain amount of quiet time each day to reflect on Allah (SWT) and the Hereafter, we increase our mindfulness. We become aware of His presence, increase our gratitude for the favors we receive from Him, and prepare for the life to come.

Such a form of meditation can be enhanced by reading the Quran and is one of the best exercises for mindfulness.

*"It is a Book full of blessings which We have sent down to
you, that they may ponder its verses, and that those who are
understanding may be admonished."*
[Surah Ṣād 38:29]

Al-Amanah (Honesty):
Be Truthful and Trustworthy

"The greatest truth is honesty; the greatest falsehood is dishonesty."

[Abū Bakr Siddiq]

The Arabic word for honesty is ‹Amanah›, which means trustworthy. It involves giving people their rights and returning what you have with you and preserving those rights for them. Prophet Muḥammad ﷺ was an ideal example of trustworthiness and honesty, which is why he was also called the truthful one (As-Ṣādiq) and the trustworthy one (Al-Amīn).

Honesty is one of the best manners. It shows our love for Allah (SWT) and guarantees respect for our fellow human beings. Our utterances and actions should always be in accordance with what is in our heart. Honesty is based on love of truth and gives strength, confidence, and self-confidence to the sincere person. A liar, on the other hand, must always be afraid that his lies will be exposed, and he will be despised by others if the truth comes out. Telling the truth without changing or distorting it can also be called truthfulness.

Abdullah ibn Mas‘ud reported:

> *The Prophet ﷺ said, "You must be truthful. Verily, truthfulness*
> *leads to righteousness and righteousness leads to Paradise.*
> *A person remains truthful and promotes honesty until he is*
> *recorded as truthful with Allah. And beware of falsehood.*
> *Verily, falsehood leads to wickedness, and wickedness leads to*
> *hellfire. A person continues to tell lies and encourages falsehood*
> *until he is recorded with Allah as a liar."*
> **[Ṣaḥīḥ Al-Būkhārī 6094, Ṣaḥīḥ Muslim 2607]**

Honesty is even more far-reaching than truthfulness, as it also means returning debts and rights to their owners. Likewise, there is honesty in faith, in responsibility, in work, in keeping promises, in an evaluation, in keeping secrets, and in trade.

"May Allah reward the truthful for their truthfulness and
punish the hypocrites if He wills, or turn to them in mercy.
Verily, Allah is Oft-Forgiving, Most Merciful."
[Surah Al-Aḥzāb 33:24]

Regarding our relationship with Allah (SWT), honesty goes a step further. Here our intention also plays a role. This is because to be pleasing to Allah (SWT), not only should our deeds be pure but also our intentions behind them. Allah (SWT) only accepts those deeds from us that are meant for Him, and we do not intend to please anyone else with them.

Our sincerity also extends not only to certain deeds, but to our daily lives. Whether we are a doctor, an engineer, a craftsman, a scientist, a politician, or a merchant, in all our works and deeds we can show our sincerity and our effort to do our best. Allah (SWT) observes over us and knows what we do. That is where every word and deed counts, big or small.

"I heard the Prophet ﷺ say, ‹Any man whom Allah has given
the authority to rule over some people, but he does not take care
of them honestly, will not even feel the smell of Paradise.›"
[Ṣaḥiḥ Al-Bukhārī , transmitted by Ma'qil]

In a world, where lies are becoming more and more obvious and deceit is rampant, it appears that the honest man is the fool. Therefore, it is certainly difficult to stick to the truth and remain honest.

But the Prophet ﷺ said, "If honesty is lost, then wait for ‹the Hour› (the Day of Judgment)." They asked, "How will sincerity be lost, O Messenger of Allah?" He replied, "If authority is given to those who do not deserve it, then wait for ‹the Hour› (the Day of Judgment)." **[Ṣaḥīḥ Al-Būkhārī)**

"O you who believe! Fear Allah and be with the truthful!"

"O you who believe! Fear Allah and be with the truthful!"
[Surah at-Tawbah 9:119)

Diqa (Accuracy): Success Through Punctuality

The Prophet ﷺ said, "Verily, Allah has prescribed Ihsan
(excellence) in all things."
[Ṣaḥīḥ Muslim]

Ihsan also includes being on time. When we agree to be in a place at a certain time, it is comparable to a promise. If we do not keep our promises, we are hypocrites.

*The Prophet ﷺ described one of the characteristics of a
hypocrite: "When he promises, he breaks his promise."*
[Ṣaḥiḥ Al-Būkhārī and Ṣaḥīḥ Muslim]

*"Indeed, whoever fulfills his commitments and fears Allah,
Allah loves the pious."*
[Surah Āl ʿImrān 3:76]

Allah (SWT) loves those who keep their promises. If we organize our daily activities better, we can be on time and have more time to complete our tasks. At the same time, it proves our trustworthiness and reliability at work and opens more doors for us.

In our daily life, it can always happen that we are late due to contractual matters as by our job.

Finally, Allah (SWT) also says in the Holy Quran:

"O you who believe! Fulfill your commitments."
[Surah Al-Ma'idah 5:1]

Any undue delay due to laziness, sloth, and lack of organization is a sin.

Punctuality is an important quality. It brings credibility and respect and builds positive character. It allows us to live a peaceful and productive life that makes us satisfied and happy because we do not need to feel frustrated or guilty. If we schedule our appointments and activities on time and show up early, we also do not get stressed and rushed. We have time to relax and can achieve success at the same time.

Of course, this also applies to the observance of daily prayers. This is because it is not enough to just believe in Allah (SWT), but we should also practice what we have been guided to do. If we are not punctual in our prayers, we lose their benefit.

"… Indeed, prayer is obligatory for the believers at specific times."
[SurahAn-Nisā' 4:103]

For our success, observing the daily five prayers at their appointed times is essential. For this, we should schedule our other duties and tasks around the prayer times and make a realistic plan for our worldly and religious duties without one of them overlapping with the other.

The Prophet ﷺ said, "The best deeds are the most regular ones, even if they are few."
[Ibn Mājah and Musnad-e-Aḥmad]

One of the methods of managing one's time properly is to get up early and sleep early, for the early hours bring great blessings. Starting the day with prayer brings us the grace of Allah (SWT).

When asked the Prophet ﷺ, what action was best, he replied, "Keeping the prayers at their appointed times, being dutiful to parents, and striving in the way of Allah (great jihad)."
[Ṣaḥiḥ Al-Būkhārī]

If we waste time, then we are misusing our lives. To give real value to our lives, we must give due importance to time. If we are late for a meeting and make others wait for us, we are responsible for causing them to lose valuable time because of us. This is disrespectful and does not show good manners.

The Prophet ﷺ said, "The best among you are those who have the best manners and the best character."
[Ṣaḥīḥ Al-Būkhārī]

Taharah (Cleanliness):
Keep Yourself Pure

"Verily, Allah loves those who turn to Him in repentance and
purify themselves."
[Surah Al-Baqarah 2:222]

Allah loves cleanliness and our purity. The Arabic word ‹Taharah›
literally means ‹purity from bodily impurities›. Our purification

is not only desirable, but essential for every true Muslim.

The Prophet ﷺ said, "Cleanliness is half of faith."
[Ṣaḥīḥ Muslim Book 2, No. 0432]

Cleanliness affects every aspect of our lives. There are several reasons why cleanliness is so important.

1. Cleanliness as a part of faith

We can show good manners and respect by being clean and punctual. Reverent behavior also includes ablutions (wudu) before prayer.

"…In it (the mosque) are men who love to be purified, and Allah loves those who purify themselves."
[Surah At-Taubah 9:108]

In this verse, it is emphasized that Allah (SWT) loves those who purify themselves. When we meet with our beloved, we would surely also wash ourselves thoroughly beforehand, brush our teeth, put on clean clothes, and not eat food with garlic beforehand. The way we prepare for our meetings with Allah (SWT) shows the desire we feel for Allah (SWT).

2. Cleanliness as a health and community aspect

Those who keep themselves clean and live in a clean environment are better protected against diseases of all kinds. Only when we are healthy can we understand, apply, and carry the message of Allah (SWT).

"Clean your clothes and keep away from all pollution."
[Surah Al-Muddathir 74:4]

This includes simple things such as daily brushing of teeth and body cleansing, cleanliness in cooking, washing hands before eating, taking care of clothes, cleaning the house, disposing of garbage, and keeping the surroundings such as streets and roads clean. In a clean environment, we can build healthy communities.

"You are the best community built for humanity. You enjoin what is right, and you forbid what is wrong, and you believe in Allah."
[Surah Āl ʿImrān 3:110].

3. Cleanliness for internal purification

"Allah does not intend to inconvenience you, but He intends to purify you and perfect His favor on you so that you may be thankful."
[Surah Al-Ma'ida 5:6]

Cleanliness has not only physical, but also spiritual aspects. Physical purification forms the basis for the purity of our inner self and extends to our heart, mind, and soul.

We purify ourselves from lies and hypocrisies, from bad manners, from senseless pursuit of fame, wealth, and carnal desires. The instructions of zakah (almsgiving) and fasting are nothing but purification of one's wealth and soul. At the same time, we sharpen our sense of community.

Cleanliness is the way to health and strength, for Allah (SWT) loves those who keep themselves pure. With purity of heart and mind, we can worship Allah (SWT) alone with full intention; our prayers will be accepted if we do it sincerely and with a pure heart.

Karam (Generosity):
Take the Opportunity of Giving

'Karam' is the Arabic word for generosity and is very common in Arab society. It indicates a culture of giving that is very much alive in the Islamic and Arab world. Karam is the root word for Al-Karim (The Generous), one of the 99 names of Allah (SWT), which reflects the generosity of Allah (SWT).

Prophet Muḥammad ﷺ as also known for his generosity, among his many other positive attributes.

"And You (Muhammad) are of a great moral character."
[Surah Al-Qalam 68:4]

It was narrated that after performing prayer in a mosque, the Prophet ﷺ hurriedly ran home and then returned. When asked why he had left, he replied:

"I had left a gold piece at home, which had been given to me as alms, and I disliked leaving it in my house for one night. So, I brought it to the mosque to distribute it."
[Ṣaḥiḥ Al-Būkhārī]

The concept of generosity has such a high value that it is one of the five pillars of Islam, known as Zakat (almsgiving). This involves giving a fixed portion of one's surplus money as charity to the community.

All our worldly possessions are a gift from Allah (SWT). Everything comes from Allah (SWT) and returns to Him. None of what we own will be taken with us after we die. Therefore, everything we own is only on loan. Our duty is to preserve, protect and share it. The wonderful thing about giving and sharing is that we do not have to worry about missing anything afterwards. Quite the opposite!

"And whatever good you spend, it will be repaid to you in full, and you will not be wronged."
[Surah Al Baqara 2:272]

Anything we give away generously intending to please Him, He will replace and increase. And Allah (SWT) knows what is in our hearts.

> *"Say, ‹My Lord increases the supply for His servants to whom*
> *He pleases, and restricts it for him. And whatever you spend,*
> *He will replace it for you. And He is the best of providers.›"*
> **[Surah Sabā 34:39]**

Generosity also plays an important role in business.

Abu Huraira reported:

> *The Prophet ﷺ said, "Verily, Allah loves generosity in selling,*
> *generosity in buying, and generosity in repaying."*
> **[Jāmʿi at-Tirmidhi 1319, Book 14, Ḥadīth 123]**

As for repaying, of course interest is not meant here, but that we should behave fairly and generously towards our business partners. It is also part of being a generous and honorable merchant that he does not cheat his customers in either measure or weight. Stinginess is not cool at all, even if the advertising in the media may suggest it to us. Even if we had the opportunity to push a price down because we are in a stronger bargaining position, for example, as an employer, we should always remain fair and be generous in negotiations.

As buyers, we can also show ourselves to be generous by supporting people who are trying to make an honest living with their small businesses. We can consider it a form of sadaqah to buy something from them, even though it may be a little cheaper elsewhere.

"The believer is simple and generous, but the profligate is deceitful and ignoble." **[Abu Dawud]**

Generosity is a wise investment in our future, by which we pave the way to Paradise and are rewarded with something greater than money. Therefore, it is not a chore but a great opportunity for us. Even in the greatest need, we can be generous, benevolent, and selfless, whether with our possessions or our time. By doing so, we not only prove our compassion for others, but also show Allah (SWT) our love and unwavering faith in Him. For it is Allah (SWT) who provides for us every day.

Jamal (Beauty):
Express Your Beauty

---

*The Prophet ﷺ said, "Verily, Allah is beautiful, and He loves
beauty. He loves the most sublime affairs and disapproves of
pettiness."*
[Ṣaḥīḥ Al-Albānī]

One of the 99 names of Allah (SWT) is "The Most Beautiful" (al-Jamil). Allah (SWT) is beautiful, and He loves beauty, and He wants us to be beautiful and make us beautiful. The Holy Quran emphasizes the beauty of the universe as proof of its divine origin. This is also the spiritual basis of Islamic art, which finds expression in writing (calligraphy), architecture, and the spoken word such as the recitation of the Qur'an.

‹Beauty is the splendor of truth›, is a profound quote from the famous Greek philosopher Plato. Everything that is true is also beautiful. This is true for the whole creation as well as for our soul. A true heart that can love unconditionally is the highest form of beauty.

Everything we see in nature is beautiful. Wherever we go, it is beautiful. The forests, the deserts, majestic mountains, and the vast sea – all these are forms of beauty; all plants, flowers, and animals also have their beauty.

Ugliness is an invention of human beings, and we have the choice to make our soul beautiful or ugly. From our soul emerges what we say, whether beautiful or ugly words, with which we ultimately make our inner being visible.

In our everyday lives, we often encounter people who look good on the outside, but something about their character repels us. Conversely, the same is true for people who may not look so good but seem beautiful to us because of their positive traits. These positive personality traits include cheerfulness, warmth, altruism, and optimism. When we distinguish between physical beauty and personality, we tend to appreciate people who possess such positive traits and a pure soul. The longer we know a person, the more external attributes fade. Therefore, we also say beauty is in the eye of the beholder because what is beautiful and what is not cannot be said unequivocally and is very individual.

Physical beauty is a blessing, but it is comparable to other material and transient attributes such as wealth and profession. Our current culture exaggerates physical beauty beyond its true meaning, so many people base their self-worth on whether their appearance meets the current ideal of beauty. True beauty, however, is what we carry with us in good deeds and in our soul on our spiritual journey to the afterlife.

This does not mean that we should not make ourselves beautiful. Quite the contrary. The following verse indicates to us that we also show our love and gratitude to Allah (SWT) by dressing neatly when we enter a mosque:

> *"O Children of Adam! Dress properly at every place of worship…"*
> ***[Surah Al-ʿĀrāf 7:31]***

Being close to Allah (SWT) and following His commandments creates both inner and outer beauty. Our words, character, and deeds are what truly make us beautiful. If we want to attain the nearness and love of Allah (SWT), it is by expressing His eternal beauty in us.

Al-Umm & Alab:
Honor Mother and Father

We know how important it is to show good manners, mindfulness, respect, and generosity towards our fellow human beings. In doing so, we are all too quick to forget the people closest to us, our mother (Arabic: Al-Umm) and father (Arabic: Al-abb).

"And serve Allah and set nothing aside for Him; be good to parents …"
[SurahAn-Nisā' 4:36]

The Prophet ﷺ repeatedly reminded his followers of the obligation to be good to one's parents and to show them a similar degree of kindness and love as towards Allah (SWT) – without worshiping them, of course.

"I know of no other deed that brings people closer to Allah than kind treatment and respect towards one's mother."
[Ṣaḥiḥ Al-Būkhārī 1/45]

Special attention and gratitude are given to the mother, since it is she who has taken upon herself the hardships of childbirth and weaning, and all kindness is due to her. This is appreciated in the following verse:

"And We have the entrusted human being with care for his parents. His mother carried him through hardships upon hardships, and his weaning requires two years. Be grateful to Me and to your parents; to Me is the return home."
[Surah Luqmān 31:14]

The prominent position of the mother is also vividly described in the following conversation:

A man came to the Prophet ﷺ and asked, "O Messenger of Allah! Who among the people justifies the best company from

me?" He ﷺ replied, "Your mother." The man asked, "Who then?" To which he ﷺ replied: "Your mother." Thereupon the man asked, "Who then?" Thereupon, the Prophet ﷺ answered again, "Your mother." Thereupon, the man asked, "Then who?" To which he ﷺ replied: "Then your father."
[Ṣaḥīḥ Al-Būkhārī 5971 and Ṣaḥīḥ Muslim 7/2]

Our mothers usually bear the greatest burden and responsibility in the family and have to face many difficulties for several years. Therefore, she especially deserves our gratitude and kindness. What kindness means in this sense was explained by the scholar Ibn al-Jawzi:

"Being kind to one's parents means: obeying them when they command you to do something, unless it is something Allah has forbidden; giving their commands priority over voluntary acts of worship; abstaining from what they forbid you to do; caring for them; serving them; approaching them with gentle humility and mercy; not raising your voice in front of them; nor directing your gaze at them; nor calling them by their names; and being patient with them."
[Birr al-Walidayn]

Of course, this does not apply in exceptional cases where parents harm their children, which, of course, is not to be tolerated. But in normal cases, it is true that we are loved by our parents, and we should ask ourselves if our behavior towards them is appropriate.

The Prophet ﷺ said that kindness to parents is among the best deeds, just as disobedience to them is among the greatest sins.

*"The greatest sins are joining partners with Allah in worship, being
ungrateful or unloving to one's parents, killing a soul forbidden by
Allah, and bearing false witness."*
[Ṣaḥiḥ Al-Būkhārī]

The unique position of mothers is proven to us by the Prophet ﷺ
in his words:

"Paradise is at the feet of your mother."
**[Musnad-e-Aḥmad, Sunan An-Nasā'i, Sunan Ibn
Mājah]**

Allah (SWT) is very concerned that we serve our parents and
make them proud of us. By showing them kindness and obedience,
protecting them, and showing them our love, we also gain the love of
Allah (SWT), His mercy and good blessings.

26

Rukhsa (Relief):
Accept the Relief of Allah

"Allah will lighten your burden, for man is created weak."
[Surah An-Nisā' 4:28]

Whether it is learning patience, repentance, generosity, mindfulness, charity, self-control, and other positive character traits, in our pursuit of excellence, we know that we have Allah (SWT) on our side. And He is Loving, Merciful and Generous. He would rather not bully us and make our lives unnecessarily difficult.

> *"Allah wants to make things easy for you, He would rather not make things difficult ..."*
> **[Surah Al-Baqarah 2:185]**

And the Prophet ﷺ said,

> *"The Deen (faith/religion) is easy ..."*
> **[Ṣaḥiḥ Al-Būkhārī]**

Allah (SWT) does not burden a soul beyond its capacity. There will always be challenges, temptations, and difficulties in our lives, but they are things that we can ultimately endure while learning to cope with them.

At the same time, we are also comforted. Surah Ash-Sharh (literally, ‹comfort›) was revealed before Prophet Muḥammad ﷺ emigrated from Makkah to Madīnah. It was meant to comfort and encourage him as one who had to endure the most hostility, criticism, insults, and ridicule.

> *"And, verily, with hardships comes ease."*
> **[Surah Ash-Sharh 94:5]**

In this Surah, Allah (SWT) promises that with every difficulty, there is also relief so that our lives become easier. Especially when we go through dark phases of life, it is important to know that we will receive comfort and encouragement to boost our morale. No burden is so heavy that we cannot bear it.

The Prophet ﷺ said, "Allah has not sent me to cause worry, to cause trouble, or to want to cause trouble. Allah has sent me to teach and to make things easy ..."
[Muslim; transmitted by Abu Huraira]

Compared to the mercy of Allah (SWT), all our difficulties, problems, and challenges are not insurmountable. There is always a solution to an issue. All we have to do is to keep our faith in Him and follow His path with patience and righteousness.

The other wonderful message is that Allah (SWT) gives us ease so that our lives become easier. And most of all, Allah (SWT) loves it when we accept His facilitation and do not reject them.

The Prophet ﷺ said, "Allah, the Exalted, loves it when His facilitations are accepted, just as He dislikes it when one disobeys Him."
[Musnad-e-Ahmad]

This ḥadīth shows Allah (SWT)'s mercy towards His servants and that He loves it when we accept His reliefs. They are like indirect gifts. When we give a gift to a person, our most beautiful thanks are what we get back when the recipient accepts our gift and is happy about it. We make other people happy by accepting their gifts, whether it is something big or small. The real gift is the love that motivates the giving, not the value of the gift.

Allah (SWT) also wants us to follow His facilitation. Because by doing so, we prove our humility and gratitude to Him. An example of relief was revealed in Surah Al-Baqarah.

"Ramadan is the month in which the Quran was revealed.
Guidance for humanity, and clear portents of guidance, and the
Criterion. Whoever of you witnesses the month, shall fast it.
But whoever is sick, or on a journey, then several other days.
God desires ease for you, and does not desire hardship for you,
that you may complete the number, and celebrate God for having
guided you so that you may be thankful."
[Surah Al-Baqarah 2:185]

When we are sick or traveling, we should not fast during this time, but on other days. This will make it easier for us to fast in these situations. We can therefore gain Allah (SWT)'s love by gratefully heeding His Divine benefits and comforts.

Qudwa: Take the Prophet Muhammad as a Role Model

"Say, ‹If you love Allah, then follow me (Prophet Muhammad) thus Allah will love you and will forgive you your sins. Allah is Oft-Forgiving and Most Merciful.›"
[Surah Āl ʿImrān 3:31]

The life of the Prophet ﷺ is full of impressive examples that show that he is a perfect role model in his ethical behavior and teachings for every person who strives for a virtuous life.

"And you are of a great moral character."
[Surah al-Qalam 68:4]

Nearly every human being seeks role models throughout his life and tries to imitate their behavior or way of life. What distinguishes Prophet Muḥammad ﷺ from other role models is the fact that his exemplary behavior was not limited to one or a few characteristics.

He was excellent in all human qualities, be it his patience, generosity, piety, honesty, modesty, justice or humility, as well as his exquisite humor and lightheartedness to his exquisite manners. The list of the incomparable qualities of the Prophet ﷺ is almost endless.

Thus, Prophet Muḥammad ﷺ is the best role model for every aspect of our lives. From the Aḥadīth, we can see how the Quran lived in practice. The Sunnah (the practice of the Prophet) concerns every part of life, such as faith, worship, morals, and ethics.

Allah (SWT) says in the Quran:

"Verily, you have in the Messenger of Allah a good example for everyone who hopes in Allah and the Last Day and remembers Allah frequently."
[Surah Ahzāb 33:21]

When we compare our lives with that of the Prophet ﷺ, we quickly realize the great discrepancy. We may wonder if we could ever be like the Prophet ﷺ, regardless of how hard we try to practice kindness, gentleness, diligence, praise, patience, and other qualities.

How impatient we are, often when our counterpart holds a different opinion that does not correspond to ours. Prophet Muḥammad ﷺ had angelic patience with all his adversaries, who kept putting great obstacles in his way. His patience with them sometimes dragged on for years. Nevertheless, he remained kind and gracious to them and even offered supplications on their behalf. In his self-sacrifice and generosity, too, few may surpass him. He put the needs of others before his own and could refuse anything to those who wanted something from him. He preferred to part with everything he had to provide for the poor while living impoverished himself. At the same time, he was a great father, husband, leader, teacher, and preacher.

The Prophet ﷺ said, "The one of you who is closest to me on the Day of Judgment will be the one who has the best character."
(Ṣaḥīḥ Al-Būkhārī)

Even if we will not attain all the qualities of the Prophet ﷺ in their perfection, we should sincerely and wholeheartedly try to follow the Prophet ﷺ because that is Ihsan, our pursuit of perfection.

"If you avoid from the worst of what you are forbidden, then We will take away your lesser evils from you and guide you to an honorable place." **(SurahAn-Nisā' 4:31)**

Allah (SWT) is the Merciful and Kind. He sees everything, including our efforts and whether we avoid the major sins. Allah loves us and sees past our weaknesses if we make Prophet Muḥammad ﷺ the model of our lives.

28

Masjid (Mosque): The House of Allah

"And the places of worship belongs to Allah. So do not call on anyone besides Allah."
[Surah Al-Jinnn, 72:18]

The mosque is the house of Allah (SWT), where He is worshiped and glorified, whether through prayers, reciting the Qur'an, remembering Him, or other good deeds. Here we can approach Allah (SWT) uniquely.

Abu Huraira reported:

The Prophet ﷺ said, "The most beloved places with Allah
are the mosques, and the most hated places with Allah are the
markets."
[Ṣaḥīḥ Muslim 671]

Mosques are places of worship of Allah (SWT) alone, free from idolatrous practices. They are Allah (SWT)'s the most beloved places. If we want to gain the love of Allah (SWT), we should make what Allah (SWT) loves our heart's desire. Of course, people can meet in other places to pray together or even alone at home. But communal prayer in a mosque has a special significance, as we can see from the following ḥadīth:

"Prayer in community is superior to prayer alone by twenty-
seven degrees."
[Ṣaḥīḥ Būkhārī 1064]

During the daily obligatory prayer (Namāz) and prostration (Sajdah), we are always close to Allah (SWT) Almighty.

"By no means! Do not obey him. But prostrate and be come
near (to Allah)!"
[Surah Al-ʿAlaq 96:19]

Mosques also have other qualities. They are meeting places for our Muslim community, where religious classes are held, where we gather to exchange and discuss ideas, and where we learn about important religious events and duties. They are the center of our community. Therefore, we should consider the House of Allah (SWT) as the most significant home in our lives and – whenever possible – prefer to pray here in the community rather than alone.

The Prophet ﷺ said, "The mosque is the home of every righteous person. Allah Almighty has guaranteed the spirit, mercy, and safe passage across the bridge of Hell to those who make their home in the mosques for the pleasure of Allah Almighty."
[Shu'ab al-Īmān 2689]

The mosques are exclusively for the remembrance of Allah (SWT), prayer, knowledge, good lessons, and the gathering of the Muslim community.

Buraydah reported:

"A man announced loudly in the mosque, ‹Has anyone seen my red camel?› The Prophet ﷺ said, ‹May you don't find it!› Verily, the mosques were built only for the purpose for which they were built."
[Ṣaḥīḥ Muslim 569]

Certainly, trade should not be conducted in a mosque, and it should not be turned into a marketplace. This is because a marketplace usually does not emanate positive energy. There, people haggle, deceive, and make false promises. There, we quickly forget our prayers and buy things we do not need, fueling our addiction to materialism and greed. Occasionally, it is also a waste of time that we could better spend on other and more productive endeavors. In any case, it is difficult to remember Allah (SWT) in a marketplace, so we can quickly forget our true purpose for being.

It was reported that Salman Al-Farsi (R.A.) said, "I heard the Prophet ﷺ say, ‹Whoever goes to morning prayer first thing in the morning goes out with the banner of faith, but whoever goes to the marketplace first thing in the morning goes out under the banner of Iblis (Satan).›"
[Sunan Ibn Mājah Ḥadīth 2234]

Besides getting closer to Allah (SWT) during our prayers in a mosque, we even get another promise:

The Prophet ﷺ said, "Whoever goes to the mosque in the morning or in the evening, Allah prepares for him a place in Jannah (Paradise) whenever he goes to the mosque in the morning and returns from it in the evening."
[Rīyāḍ as-Ṣāliḥīn 1053]

29

Al hub fi Allah:
Loving for Allah

"You are the best community that ever emerged for humanity."
[Surah Āl 'Imrān 3:10]

The word ‹love› is used in our vernacular in different situations. For example, we speak of ‹great love› when we are in love with another person and feel that we are soul mates and belong together. We also know the term concerning ‹mother love›, the strong emotional bond a mother has with her biological children. And then there are the many events, situations, and things, be it a movie, food, a piece of music, a trip, or a book, that excite us so much that we declare to love this or that. Often this is followed directly by the reasoning: ‹I love it / her / him because ...›

‹Loving for Allah (SWT)› (Arabic: Al Ḥub Fī Allāh) has a slightly different meaning, namely loving someone for the sake of Allah (SWT). This is done in two ways: in the heart and through deeds.

We love someone for Allah (SWT) in our heart because of their relationship with Allah (SWT). This starts with loving Allah (SWT), the Prophet, the Messengers, and everyone who follows them. It is a love that we have in our heart for other Muslims. We see the other as a comrade, a good friend, and a companion, especially within the Ummah, the Islamic community. We do not harbor any anger or other negative feelings towards each other. Even if we come from different families and home countries, and have different skin colors or nationalities, whether we are Arabs, Americans, Indians, French or Germans, we are brothers and sisters.

Outwardly, we show this love for Allah (SWT) through corresponding good deeds. We are there for each other, we support each other, we help each other with problems in everyday life and offer our help or visit each other. Of course, the good deeds also apply to non-Muslims. To the brothers and sisters of our Deen (faith), we should furthermore show special love for Allah (SWT).

The Prophet ﷺ said, "Whoever possesses the following three
qualities will taste the sweetness of faith:

1.　the one who loves Allah and His Messenger more than

anything else.

2. *who loves a person and loves him only for Allah.*

3. *who hates to return to disbelief (atheism) after Allah has delivered (saved) him from it, as he hates to be thrown into the Fire."*

[Ṣaḥiḥ Al-Būkhārī 21]

Life in modern times is covered with difficulties, challenges, and worries. As a result, more and more people are only interested in themselves and perhaps their closest circle. How their Muslim brothers and sisters are doing is indifferent to them. Therefore, love for Allah (SWT) is even more important today so that selfishness cannot spread any further. Islam has managed to unite us. We are like the fingers of one hand. When we cover the palm, the fingers appear separate from each other. But underneath, we are connected to each other. And when one part of us suffers, we all suffer. Just when one of us is suffering, we should show them our love and care, ask if they need anything, and ask about their welfare. If we are the best community that has been brought forth, then we must live that in word and deed and strengthen our bond with each other.

The Prophet ﷺ said, "Allah (s.w.t.) said, ‹Those who love one another for My sake will stand on pedestals of light, and the prophets and martyrs will envy them (i.e., wish that they receive the same).›"

[Jāmiʿ at-Tirmidhi 2390]

A special power of our attachment has the following sentence, ‹I love you for the sake of Allah.› (Arabic: to a man ‹Uḥibbuka fi-allāhi or to a woman ‹Uḥibbuki fi-allāhi). This may feel strange at first to say these words, especially to people we do not know or are not related to. But should we miss this chance of blessing and not say these strong words?

The Prophet ﷺ said, "If one of you loves his brother, he should tell him."

[Jāmʿi at-Tirmidhi]

Loving a person for the sake of Allah (SWT) means to consider him as a part of a big whole, and to offer him help to support in case of problems. And it means not stirring up hatred against him, even if he disagrees on some things. This means loving for Allah (SWT). We are the best community and Allah (SWT) has distinguished us with this quality. And it is associated with His love and blessings.

The Prophet ﷺ said, "A man was visiting his brother in another city. And Allah assigned an angel to wait for him on his way. When he came to him, the angel asked, ‹Where do you intend to go?› The man replied, ‹I intend to go to my brother in this city.› The angel asked, ‹Have you done him any favor (that you intend to return)?› He replied, ‹No, only that I love him for the sake of Allah, the Exalted and Glorious.› Thereupon the angel said, ‹I am a messenger of Allah who tells you that Allah loves you as you love Him.›"

[Ṣaḥīḥ Muslim No. 6226]

30

Thabat:
With Constancy to the Goal

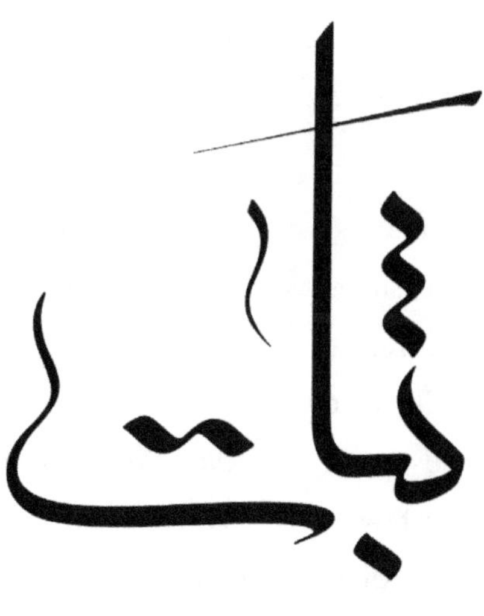

We are all on an individual spiritual journey to love Allah (SWT) Almighty. It is a journey of our heart that knows and loves Allah (SWT).

The Prophet ﷺ said, "There is a piece of flesh in the body, if it becomes good (improved), the whole body becomes good, but if it becomes spoiled, the whole body becomes spoiled. And that is the heart."
[Ṣaḥīḥ Al-Būkhārī, 52]

And the Prophet ﷺ taught us that of all our attributes, Allah (SWT) is mostly concerned about the condition of our heart.

"Verily, Allah does not look at your bodies, nor at your faces, but He looks at your hearts," and he pointed to the heart with his fingers.
[Ṣaḥīḥ Muslim 2564b]

If we want to achieve something in our lives, regardless of the areas, we must remain steadfast and constant at it. This is the only way we can improve ourselves. For example, if we would like to learn a new language, it will not do us much good if we try to memorize 1000 vocabulary words in a single day. We are much more successful if we regularly learn a few new words. When we sow seeds, we must give water and take care of them regularly so that beautiful plants will grow from them.

Furthermore, the purpose of Ramadan is not that we remember Allah (SWT) for a month and do good deeds, then check it off after Eid and continue our lives as we did before Ramadan. Rather, the month of Ramadan is a month of training where we focus on increasing our good deeds as we become less distracted. And we are prepared to maintain our faith even in difficult times.

The key to any success is consistency (Arabic: Thabat), no matter how arduous the path to the goal. This also applies to our journey to Allah (SWT). Occasionally, we simply succeed in staying on the right path with our hearts. At other times, we allow ourselves to become numbed by the material world and become preoccupied with the many desires of ourselves. In the process, we lose focus so that a veil settles over our hearts, and we find it increasingly difficult to distinguish the true from the false. We then become discouraged and feel that we may never make it.

But we should never forget that Allah (SWT) is always close to us and waiting for us to return to Him. Constancy helps us in purifying and keeping our hearts clean. With time, it becomes easier and builds up to Ihsan (excellence).

> *The Prophet ﷺ was asked, "What deeds are most loved by Allah?" He replied, "The most regular, consistent deeds, even if they are few." And he added, "Take upon yourselves only those deeds which are within your means."*
> **[Ṣaḥiḥ Al-Bukhārī 6465]**

It is like many other things: once we are used to them, they come easily to us. But how can we achieve consistency to remain continuous and steady in our journey to Allah (SWT)?

As the Prophet ﷺ explained to us, we can improve even a few things that do not overwhelm us and make small but consistent changes in our lives. The only important thing is that we keep them consistent.

This is where the many routines, such as daily prayers, help us as Muslims because we are very fortunate to be equipped with such a structure for our lives that keeps our lifestyle in a healthy routine. So, a first step could be to stop missing any of the five daily prayers and to be punctual.

> *"… Indeed, prayer is obligatory for the believers at specific times."*
> **[Surah An-Nisā', 4:103]**

Depending on where we are in our journey, there are many other ways to incorporate routines into our lives. This can be keeping a gratitude journal, reciting the Quran repeatedly, fasting for Allah (SWT) regularly, supporting a poor person repeatedly, performing night prayer continuously, visiting a mosque regularly to pray in community, or strengthening our relationship with our parents.

The ways to purify one's heart and train one's character are unlimited. We can take some of the good deeds we do in Ramadan and keep them throughout the year or throughout our lives.

> *"As for those who strive for us; We will surely guide them to Our ways. And verily, Allah is with those who do good."*
> **[Surah al-'Ankabūt 29:69]**

If we move forward and sincerely repent of our mistakes, Allah (SWT) will guide us to the best path. Therefore, we should continue to strive to purify our hearts, have positive intentions, and continually improve our level of piety.

May Allah (SWT) bless you and help us all to consistently continue our journey to Him to attain His love and enter the Eternal Paradise.

Praise be to Allah (SWT), the Lord of the Worlds, who guided us to Islam, and we would not have been guided if Allah (SWT) had not guided us. There is no God but Him. We ask Allah (SWT) for forgiveness and repentance. May God's peace and blessings be upon His servant and Messenger Muḥammad and upon all his relatives and companions.

Thank Allah (SWT) for the blessings of Islam. Amīn.

Imprint

Author:	Salah Moujahed
Publisher	BAAB Publishing
Editing:	Hassan Mehmood
Typesetting, Layout:	Luminousproject
Cover Design, Graphics, Calligraphy:	Oussama Senhadji
Print:	Amazon

Muslim Notebooks c/o BAAB Ltd

59, Mere Road

B23 7LL Birmingham

salah@muslimnotebooks.com

9 781915 690104